1001 Curiosities of Barcelona

Redbook

1001 Curiosities of Barcelona

Silvia Suárez and Anna-Priscila Magriñà Aguilera

MA NON TROPPO

Translation: Andrew Nicoll
Cover design: Regina Richling
Design: Amanda Martínez

ISBN: 978-84-18703-77-5
D.L.: B-2.282-2024

Reprográficas Malpe – Pol. Ind. Los Olivos
Calle de la Calidad, 34, Bloque 2 Nave 728906 Getafe, Madrid

Printed in Espanya – *Impreso en España*

Contents

Foreword

A City of Stories

The city of Barcelona is like an open book. Distributed among its streets and squares, thousands of stories lie dormant, waiting to be discovered by passers-by. The great constructions of the Middle Ages and Modernism are mixed with the memories that remain from its many wars. Over the centuries, politics has erected buildings and destroyed them, but the city has never stopped looking to the future.

The Romans made it great, but the oppression of the walls almost wiped it out. Barcelona has had brilliant moments and has fought against the injustices that have tried to degrade it. It has been a violent city and has seen the creation of unusual works of art.

Barcino, Barshaluna, Barcelona has welcomed marvellous architects, internationally famous actresses and thinkers and scientists who have always helped drive society forward with their work. While reliving the tales of the city, we will, almost without meaning to, take part in an exciting tour of the most important points in our history: the battles of counts and kings, workers' struggles, the most extraordinary discoveries and, above all, the day-to-day life of ordinary people. You see the streets of the city breathe history. It's a history brimming with anecdotes that are worth getting to know to better understand the world around us.

In Barcelona, everything begins and ends. Join us on this fascinating adventure full of curiosities that explain, to a greater or lesser extent, our way of life.

1. Curiosities of the history of Barcelona

A Retirement Home for Roman Veterans

Let me tell you a couple of cool stories about how the amazing city of Barcelona came to be. So, one tale goes back to the Roman times. It's said that the mighty Hercules sailed through a crazy storm and ended up on the Catalan coast. The locals were so impressed by him that they even named him Barca Nona, after one of his ships that sank there. Now, the other legend has a Carthaginian twist to it. It claims that Amílcar Barca, the father of the famous Hannibal, founded Barcelona way back in 230 BC. But honestly, both these stories sound a bit far-fetched.

❖ ❖ ❖

Even though the exact origins of Barcelona remain a bit murky, we do know that the Iberians, Greeks, and Carthaginians all settled in this area. Then, those Romans came along and, as they were expanding like crazy, they rebuilt the city in the late 1st century BC. Emperor Augustus said "Let's make a retirement home for our army veterans here", and he named it Iulia Augusta Faventia Paterna Barcino. So, Barcelona started off as a retirement home for Roman veterans. Can you imagine?

Remains of the Temple of Augustus.

By the way, if you ever find yourself at the *Center Excursionista de Catalunya* headquarters on Paradís Street, keep an eye out for a millstone embedded in the floor. This symbol right here is a reminder of the mountain peak called Tàber, where the Romans started building their new city. But wait till you see the four columns inside the association's walls! They were put up during the Roman Empire and are the only remains of the grand temple of Augustus that stood there when *Barcino* was born. The Romans built the city just like they did with their other settlements: straight lines and a grid pattern filled with houses and buildings.

Did you know?
Those columns, which marked one of the temple's corners, have grooves running down their shafts and fancy Corinthian capitals.

SOME INFO

Three of the columns in the Temple of Augustus have stayed put since they were built by the ancient 'Catalan' Romans. The fourth one, along with the Gothic gallery of the CEC, stood in Plaza del Rei for quite a while.

Oysters Designated as Origin Barcino

During the Roman era, people in Barcelona went crazy about oysters. But things took a drastic turn in the 19th century when brutal industrialization changed everything, even underwater. Oysters used to be so abundant back then that now you can stumble upon their shells while digging in the city. *Barcino*, the ancient name for Barcelona, had the important job of bringing together and managing a relatively small but super-productive area.

The land was so fertile that it made the territory rich. They mostly grew cereals and grapes, and they had mining resources like iron and possibly silver in the Gavà region and an abundance of seafood. These "marine goods" became so famous that even a poet named Ausonio praised the fish sauce and oysters from the area in the 4th century.

When 'Adapt or Die' Had a Literal Meaning

Roman tower close to Ramón Berenguer Square.

The Romans, being clever strategists, built a wall around *Barcino* to protect it from potential attacks. But back in those days, the saying "adapt or die" had a very literal meaning. The Romans had to upgrade their walls several times to make sure they could defend what was inside.

Barcino wasn't initially a powerful city. *Tarraco* had always been stronger from the start. However, *Barcino*'s development over the centuries was so impressive that it eventually became an important military centre during the Late Empire. It was in the 4th century that the city's long-lasting walls were built.

If you visit Ramon Berenguer El Gran square, you'll find one of the best-preserved parts of the Roman wall in the city. According to information found on a slab in Montjuïc in the 19th century assuming it's accurate, this defensive wall was built between the years 270 and 310 AD by order of the magistrate Caius Coelius. It's likely the new construction was built on top of an earlier wall.

SOME INFO

Stone blocks from Montjuïc were used to build the walls. They used the *opus quadratum* technique, where blocks were joined together with mortar and lime cement.

Did you know?
The original perimeter of the wall, which can still be seen today, was approximately 1,270 metres long.

Water Almost from the Tap

In Duran i Bas Street, you'll find four arcades integrated into a wall. These arcades are remnants of one of the two aqueducts that brought water directly from Collserola and Besòs to the Roman city.

The Graves of the Poor

Over in Madrid's Plaza Vila, there's an open-air Roman necropolis. It contains eighty-five funerary elements that were built between the 2nd and 3rd centuries. Among the remains, you can find numerous tombs that were used by the poor.

Open-air Roman necropolis in Plaza Vila of Madrid.

A Town Hall on the Site of a Mosque

When the Western Roman Empire disappeared in 476, lots of Germanic folks saw a chance to grab some land that had no owner. So, after some battles, the Visigoths under Ataúlfo ended up taking control of most of the Iberian Peninsula, while the Franks claimed the Gallic territories.

❖ ❖ ❖

Ataúlfo, king of the Visigoths.

Painting depicting the Battle of Guadalete between the Visigoths and the Muslims.

Then, in 711, the Muslims arrived on the Iberian Peninsula and defeated the Visigoths in the Battle of Guadalete. The new invaders managed to settle all over the place, except for a small stronghold in the north, which is present-day Asturias. It was from there that the Reconquest, as it came to be known, began years later. The Visigothic rule was over, and the Muslim era, known as Al-Andalus, began, lasting for nearly a century in Barcelona.

The new conquerors changed the name of Barcelona to *Madinat Barshaluna*. However, in terms of urban development, not much progress was made during this period. The newcomers destroyed the Palau Reial Major and a significant number of Christian churches. They used the vacant spaces to build mosques. Some historians suggest that the main mosque was built on the very spot where Barcelona City Hall would later be constructed in 1369. Can you imagine a grand mosque standing where the council stands today?

The First Count of Barcelona: A Lord from Carcassonne

In ancient Gaul, the Merovingian dynasty was replaced by the Carolingian. Charlemagne, who belonged to the Carolingian dynasty, wanted to reclaim the Western Roman Empire. So, in 800, he became emperor. A year later, the Franks took control of Barshaluna, and Charlemagne decided to incorporate the city into the Hispanic March.

❖ ❖ ❖

The Hispanic March was a territory divided into counties, created to protect the Frankish empire from foreign attacks.

Meanwhile, a nobleman from Carcassonne named Guifred the Hairy showed great bravery and loyalty to the Carolingian monarchs. As a reward for his deeds in battle, he was made the Count of Urgell, La Cerdanya, and Conflent. Over time, his territory expanded to include Barcelona and Girona, consolidating most of the counties of the Hispanic March under his rule. Until then, the Franks had personally chosen the first eleven counts of the Hispanic March. But under Guifred, the position of count became hereditary, and thus, the House of Barcelona dynasty began.

The Legend of the Four Bars

Count Guifred the Hairy played a significant role in the emergence of one of Catalonia's most famous legends: the birth of the four bars, which would later become the emblem of Catalonia. Guifred already had a coat of arms. This one was golden and without a design, too simple for a noble's taste. But when

The painting shows the moment when Lluís the Pious draws the four bars with Guifred the Hairy's blood.

Guifred the Hairy's tomb can be found in the monastery of Santa Maria de Ripoll.

he got seriously hurt in a battle, protecting the Carolingians' interests, Charlemagne's son, Lluís the Pious 778-840, put his fingers in Hairy's wound and made four lines on the yellow shield using the count's blood. The Frankish king wanted to honour Wilhelm's bravery against his foes with this cool new symbol. And that's how the four bars came to be.

SOME INFO

The so-called Catalunya Vella (Old Catalonia) was born from the Hispanic March.

A Very Romanesque Monastery

At the end of Sant Pau Street, in the Raval neighbourhood, you'll find the old Benedictine monastery of Sant Pau del Camp. People think it got its name because it was built outside the city walls, out in the countryside. Inside the monastery, there's a tombstone from way back in 911, marking the resting place of Guifred II, The Hairy's son. The place has had a tough time, though. It was destroyed in 985 when the Muslim leader al-Mansur attacked, and later, it was looted by the Almoravids too. They rebuilt the church around 1117, using the Lombard Romanesque style.

Cloister of the monastery of Sant Pau del Camp, at the end of Sant Pau Street in Barcelona.

About Vocabulary
Presumably The Hairy's count had a good natural protection for the harshest winters in 9th century Barcelona.

When the Laziness of the Franks Delivered Barcelona's Independence

The counties' hereditary principle started with Guifred the Hairy, but it was not until Borrell II 947-992 that the House of Barcelona stopped being under the Frankish Crown's control.

❖ ❖ ❖

In 985, the Muslims realized the potential of the maritime city and came back to Catalan lands with al-Mansur at their head. They occupied the city for only a few months, and even though the Franks were supposed to help Barcelona when it was in danger, they didn't lift a finger to protect it from the new attackers. This made the Catalan count decide to stop paying homage to the new Frankish king since the pact was broken, and the Carolingian dynasty was gone. As a result, the House of Barcelona started to go its own way.

Depiction of Borrell II.

Sant Jordi's Invaluable Aid

They say that Borrell II had the mighty Sant Jordi (Saint George) on his side when al-Mansur took over Barcelona. To fight against the Muslims, the count sought refuge in Montserrat and gathered an army to retake Barcelona. Borrell II, along with six loyal knights, embarked on the journey to Barcelona with their army. According to popular belief, Sant Jordi joined them, guarding them against any ill omens. With such outstanding help, it's no wonder Barcelona ended up in Christian hands once more.

Sculpture of Sant Jordi in the cloister of Barcelona Cathedral.

The Most Splendid Residence in Barcelona: El Palau Reial Major

The stairs in Plaça del Rei take you up to the Museu d'Història de la Ciutat de Barcelona Barcelona History Museum nowadays, but back in the day, it wasn't just tourists who walked on these steps. Counts and kings used to strut their stuff on these stairs because they're part of the 'architectural ensemble' of the Palau Reial Major.

❖ ❖ ❖

The famous stairs of the Plaça del Rei in Barcelona.

A Residence with Everything You Need

The Plaça del Rei complex is a huge place with four buildings: the palace itself, Tinell Hall, Palau del Lloctinent, and the Church of Santa Àgata. Legend has it that the Palau Reial was built by Athaulf, the first Visigoth king who conquered Barcelona in 415. Sadly, he was assassinated by his own people in the same year while in the city.

The Chapel of Santa Àgata is a Gothic building dating back to 1302. It was commissioned by Jaime II and his wife, Blanca of Naples, as a replacement for the old palace sanctuary. Inside, you can find the *Retablo del condestable o de la epifanía* (1464) by Jaume Huguet from Vallès, which is considered one of the finest examples of Catalan gothic painting.

The Tinell Hall, built between 1359 and 1362, is a breathtaking Gothic space that in its heyday was used for grand ceremonies in the Palace.

The Palau del Lloctinent, also known as The Lieutenant's Palace, was constructed in 1549. It was supposed to be the residence of the King of Catalonia, but it never fulfilled that role. Instead, it served as the Archive of the Crown of Aragon for many years.

From top to bottom: the Chapel of Santa Àgata, the *Retablo del condestable o de la epifanía*, Tinell Hall and the Palau del Lloctinent.

About Vocabulary
Athaulf means "noble wolf" in Germanic.

A Royal Corral for the Whole Town

The Plaça del Rei used to be part of the corral of the Palau Reial. The Catalan counts weren't into frills. They kept it simple with the palace's architecture and for a long time even let people use their corral as a market and meeting place. From the 14th century, the market moved around a bit before finally settling in La Rambla.

A Difficult Citizen to House: The Executioner

Now, right between the chapel and the museum in the Plaça del Rei, there's a glass entrance. Guess what? It's the entrance to the executioner's house. Being an executioner was a big deal – people both respected and feared him. He had a job to do, but no one really wanted to hang out with a professional killer. The people living inside the walls didn't want him nearby because he reminded them of dark memories. However, the politicians back then thought it was too harsh to make him live far away from the city since all he did was follow orders.

The executioner also lived in the palace.

> **About Vocabulary**
> The *estiracordetes* the one who pulls the strings was the name given to the executioner's assistant. Where did this character live? Your guess is as good as mine.

The problem of finding a house for the executioner became a big headache and was even discussed in the Consell de Cent. After throwing around some ideas, they finally came up with a solution. If the executioner couldn't live inside the city or outside it, they decided to make a small space for him within the walls, close to the court. And that's how they sorted it out.

The Countess Who Called the Shots

Borrell II had a son named Ramon Borrell 972-1017, and he ruled from 992 to 1017. But forget about his escapades for now because we're more interested in his wife: Ermesenda of Carcassonne 972-1057.

❖ ❖ ❖

This countess became a big deal during the Catalan Middle Ages because she didn't just want to be known as Borrell's wife. Ermesenda wanted to be involved in all the important things that were going on, so she made sure to be present for every decision that her husband made.

Ermesenda of Carcassone.

SOME INFO

Ermesenda put all her efforts into rebuilding Barcelona after al-Mansur was gone.

Did you know?
Following the custom of Visigothic law, Ramon Borrell had to give a tenth of his assets to Ermesenda at the time of their wedding. In the past, the dowry was a man's issue.

When Men Had to Pay to Get Married

In the High Middle Ages, it was the future husband who had to cough up 10% of their assets when they tied the knot. But starting from the 13th century, the tables turned and the women had to hand over a dowry when they got married. If a girl wanted to become a nun, her dowry went towards the convent she joined.

This new custom was a nightmare for parents with daughters. They had a hard time from the moment their little girls were born because their future depended largely on their dowry. No matter

what social class they were in, a woman without a dowry was headed straight for poverty or some other unpleasant fate.

Ermesenda was present for every decision her husband took.

The Eternal Regent

Ermesenda got married to Ramon Borrell I when she was just seventeen. They had three kids, but only one of them survived long enough to take power.

When the king died in 1017, Ermesenda took control of the county until her son Berenguer Ramon I came of age. She surrounded herself with smart advisors and made decisions that suited her. The only problem was her eldest child. Eventually, the day came when he claimed his inheritance: the control of the county. Ermesenda was so used to being in charge that she only handed over power to Berenguer Ramon when she realized she couldn't stay in that role anymore. But that wasn't the end for the great countess, because Ermesenda would rule again. In 1035, her son died, leaving only twelve-year-old Ramon Berenguer I as the heir.

Without wasting any time, Ermesenda reconnected with her old advisors and took charge once more. However, her grandson eventually grew up, and she was forced to leave the political stage again.

Counts Can Also Find Love From Time to Time

Ramon Berenguer I 1023-1076 had the power of the House of Barcelona under his wing. After tying the knot for a second time, the count happened to find himself in Narbonne on his way back from a trip to Rome, where he had had an audience with none other than the Pope!

The altarpiece represents Ramon Berenguer and Almodis' love for each other.

In the French city, he ran into a nobleman named Ponç de Tolosa, and more importantly, his wife, Almodis de la Marca 1020-1071. I say "more importantly" because their meeting had a huge impact on the future of the House. The stories of that time talk about love at first sight, like it was something out of a fairy tale. And maybe it was true, because the moment they laid eyes on each other, they knew they wanted to be together. But there was just one problem: both of them were already married. And let's not forget the biggest obstacle of them all: Ermesenda, the grandmother of all grandmothers.

Some people say the count kidnapped Almodis to bring her to Barcelona, while others believe it was a plan they had hatched to run away together. Whatever the truth is, their love didn't have an easy path. Not only were they seen as sinful in the eyes of God or maybe some people just wanted to hold power, but Ermesenda, being the grandmother, demanded that the Pope excommunicate her grandson and his new wife. But the couple wasn't ready to give up without a fight. And in the end, Ermesenda realized that continuing the feud could jeopardize the future of the House of Barcelona. So, she made a surprising decision: she pledged her loyalty to the marriage and retreated to Osona. That's where she eventually passed away at the age of eighty-three, in her estate in Sant Quirze de Besora.

SOME INFO

Ermesenda of Carcassone's tomb in the Cathedral of Girona.

Ermesenda was the driving force behind the first Romanesque buildings. She was all about getting those cathedrals in Girona, Vic, and Urgell built, along with the monasteries in Cuixà, Ripoll, and Sant Daniel, and the churches in Tavèrnoles, Casserres, and Cardona. You can even find her tomb in the Girona Cathedral, and guess what? That's one of the first places where you can see the four bars on the shield.

The House of Barcelona Increases Its Power

Ramon Berenguer I and Almodis de la Marca made sure the House of Barcelona dominated the other Catalan nobles. We're mentioning both of them because, just like the count's grandma, Ermesenda, Almodis also had a hand in ruling alongside her husband. These two were really crafty and managed to gather a whole bunch of supporters. And when sweet-talking wasn't enough, they just tossed a few coins at people to keep them loyal. They played their cards right and the House of Barcelona ended up having uncontested hegemony over all the Catalan counties.

The First Catalan Laws Are Quite Scary

According to tradition, Almodis, who had an impressive cultural background, apparently helped write some of the earliest *usatges* of Barcelona. These were a collection of laws that aimed to govern the feudal society in Catalonia back then. These laws ended up forming the foundation of Catalan law.

Miniature showing Ramon Berenguer and his wife Almodis on the left.

Extremely Physical Tests to Discover Adultery

Usatge says that if a husband accuses his wife of cheating, it's up to her to prove she's innocent. So, how did a woman manage to prove her loyalty to her husband back in the Middle Ages?
Well, the accused had two choices: either find someone brave enough to fight for her in a tournament or dip her hands in scalding water. They called it "The Trial of God" or "Ordalía". If the champion won or the woman's hands didn't get burned, she was declared innocent. But if the fighter lost or the accused's hands got hurt, it meant adultery was confirmed, and the lady's belongings would end up in her husband's coffers.

The tombs of Ramón Berenguer and Almodis, Barcelona Cathedral.

The Murderous Stepson

Pere Ramon, one of Ramon Berenguer's sons from his first marriage, wasn't exactly thrilled when his dad remarried. He was scared that Almodis' sons would take his place in the line of succession. So, what did he do? He went ahead and fatally poisoned his stepmother in 1071. Talk about a family drama.

This whole betrayal thing really took a toll on Ramon Berenguer. He was heartbroken by the loss of his wife and died five years later, probably from grief.

But wait, there's more! Pere Ramon didn't just get away with murder. He was put on trial, kicked out of town, and even got excommunicated by Pope Gregory VII. And guess what? He eventually met his end in battle on the border with the Muslim territories. I guess karma caught up with him.

But not everything is doom and gloom in this story. Ramon Berenguer and Almodis had twin sons who went on to have a happy ending.

The Twins Who Hated Each Other to the Death

The heirs of the county of Barcelona, now extensive and powerful, were the twin sons of Almodis de la Marca, Ramon Berenguer II (1053-1082) and Berenguer Ramon II (1053-1097).

❖ ❖ ❖

Ramon Berenguer II, also called Cabeza de Estopa on account of his reddish hair.

Now, these twins had a funny habit of swapping identities when it suited them. You know, like during exams, parties, presentations etc. But there's only one creepy story that survived about these kids of Almodis and Ramon Berenguer.

When they were born, a group of important people like bishops and high dignatories got together and decided that Ramon Berenguer, also known as Cabeza de Estopa because of his red hair, was the older one. They believed that the first baby out of the womb in the second trimester was the firstborn. So, Cabeza de Estopa got the honours. But Berenguer Ramon never quite bought into that. He knew he would always feel like the second son.

In an attempt to be good brothers, R.B. and B.R. tried to rule together. But guess what? It didn't work out. They couldn't stand each other.

Legend has it that they hated each other so much that they couldn't even sleep under the same roof, not even for short periods. So, they took turns living in the Royal Palace for six-month intervals, like it's some fancy beach house. They were all about not being in the same place at the same time.

Berenguer Ramon's Most Drastic Decision

Legend has it that Berenguer Ramon was so desperate to get his grubby hands on the reins of power, that one fine day he hatched a plan to catapult to the top. The boy, as ambitious as any, devised a simple, violent, but effective tactic: he'd kill his brother. And that was that.

The scene he chose for the murder was a hunt. Between the vegetation and long distances, B. R. hoped to be able to escape unnoticed. When the dead earl's body turned up, the murderous brother pointed the finger at the expedition's falconer.

Ramon Berenguer II's tomb can be found in the Cathedral of Girona.

Later, he settled in the Palau del Rei and, in blissful peace, he proclaimed himself count. But this peace would be over quickly for B.R. because he was obliged to fight a duel against the falconer who'd been unfairly accused. The fratricidal count lost the duel. But B. R. managed to get out of this sticky situation thanks to the Arabs. They threatened new invasions and people felt that it wasn't the best time to change leaders. Barcelona had to remain strong and stable whatever happened.

So, saved by the threat of Muslim invasion, *El Fraticida* (The Fratricide), as he had now gone down in the annals of history, reigned as regent until his death. The new count would be the son of the murdered brother, who was born shortly before his father died under such suspicious circumstances. *El Fraticida* could never free himself from the shadow of his missing twin brother altogether.

About Vocabulary
The constant repetition of names like Ramon and Berenguer, or Felipe or Carlos in other monarchies, is a thing the ruling families do to show that they've been in charge for a long time. It's like they're saying, "Look at us! We've been in power for generations!".

Ramon Berenguer III and His Horse's Controversial Tail

Ramon Berenguer III in the castle of Foix, painting by Marià Fortuny 1857.

Ramon Berenguer III (1082-1131), the son of the late Cabeza de Estopa, was quite the remarkable figure. They called him 'the Great' not only for his military skills but also because he had a knack for getting the most out of every situation.

❖ ❖ ❖

Through cunning and diplomacy, he conducted successful business deals and forged powerful alliances. He even became the count of Provence through a strategic marriage to Dulce de Provence. But before Dulce, there was María Díaz de Vivar, the daughter of El Cid Campeador, whom he married first. Unfortunately, their marriage was short-lived as María passed away shortly after.

Did you know?
Ramon Berenguer III was the first person to consider conquering the Balearic Islands, although he would have to wait several more years to accomplish this feat.

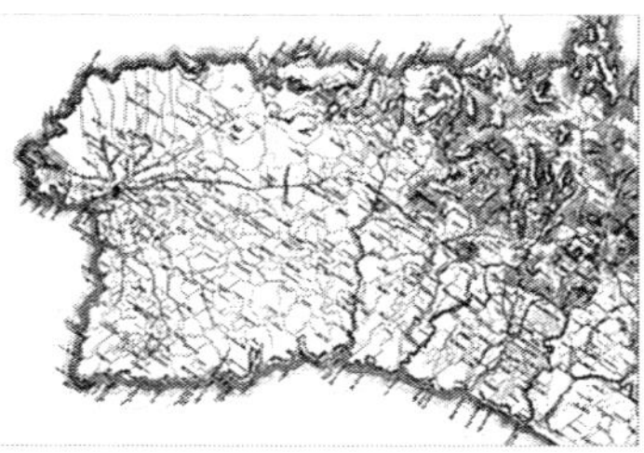

Once Upon a Time, There Was an Ugly Horse's Tail

Little did this great strategist imagine that, many years after his death, his horse's tail would cause such a stir among many people in Barcelona.

In 1888, the Barcelona City Council commissioned the sculptor Josep Llimona to create a life-size plaster sculpture of Ramon Berenguer the Great. The artwork gained immense popularity,

Josep Llimona's controversial statue restored by Frederic Marès.

and Llimona even received an award for it at the Universal Exhibition held that same year. The sculpture found its place in the statue gallery of the Palau de Bellas Artes waiting for better material. So, when they built the square named after the count, the council thought it would be the perfect spot for Llimona's statue. The only issue was that the sculptor had passed away in 1934. So, they had the idea to ask Frederic Marès, an artist, to make a bronze copy of the original statue. However, there was one small hiccup – the horse's tail that Ramon Berenguer the Great was supposed to be riding had gone missing in some forgotten warehouse at some point.

Ramon Berenguer's seal.

Because of the missing tail, Marès had to come up with a new design for the bunch of hairs, and the sculpture was finally unveiled in 1950. But as it often happens, not everyone was happy with the new tail, and there was quite an uproar among the citizens at the time.

Catalonia Can Finally Be Called Catalonia!

Ramon Berenguer III had a son named Ramon Berenguer IV. When the younger Ramon got hitched to Petronela de Aragón, something big happened. The county of Barcelona became connected to the neighbouring kingdom, and this gave birth to the Crown of Aragon.

❖ ❖ ❖

Ramon Berenguer III and Petronela of Aragón.

Now, don't get me wrong, this wasn't a full-on merger of the two dynasties. It was more like a strategic alliance. Each state maintained its own laws and boundaries, no changes there. The only addition was the introduction of a sovereign ruler, who was now called the king.

This alliance put an end to the conquest of Catalunya Nova, or New Catalonia, and allowed us to start talking about Catalonia as we know it today, with its current geographical limits.

SOME INFO

Ramon Berenguer IV (1114-1162) got married to Petronela de Aragón when he was over twenty years old and she... only one. But the marriage didn't come into effect until 1150, when the girl had just turned fourteen. Quite an age gap!

The Very First Catalan Parliament

Then came the Conqueror, the first Jaume. Thanks to him, Barcelona became a major player in Mediterranean trade, surpassing ports like Venice or Genoa.

❖ ❖ ❖

Jaume I the Conqueror, in a medieval portrait.

The monarchs of the Crown of Aragon were known for their compromise. Instead of forcing their own views on everyone, they shared power with the privileged classes of society. Up until then, they had made constant agreements with the nobility and the clergy. However, in the 13th century, a new social group emerged in the decision-making process: the bourgeoisie, which was gaining influence, particularly in Barcelona. So, where did they reach these agreements? Well, they gathered in the Catalan Courts, a medieval version of today's Parliament. The Courts were meetings between the king and representatives from three different groups. Initially, this institution only advised the monarch, but Jaime I gave it more power, and from then on, they also discussed and collaboratively created laws. In this way, they became a legislative body that decentralized power to some extent.

The Advice of Many

In 1249, after successfully taking over the Balearic Islands and the Kingdom of Valencia, Jaume I gave Barcelona the chance to govern itself with its own representatives. To make this happen, the count-king set up the basic framework for the city's municipal government: initially, there would be a council consisting of four magistrates. However, around ten years later, significant changes were made, and the council expanded to include eight councillors. The councillors' main task was to select another council of two hundred advisors. This group would later evolve into what we now know as the Consell de Cent.

El Consell de Cent (Council of One Hundred), nowadays.

Way Too Many People Here

There were about a hundred people from the nobility, and the other hundred were picked by the guilds or, you know, the upper class of the city. It was the rich merchants and well-off artisans who got to have a say and vote. But somewhere along the line, we lost a hundred of those two hundred people. And over time, only half of the original bunch made it through. That's why it got the name that stuck with us to this day.

Every year, new members were chosen and split into four groups of twenty-five. Each group had a huge responsibility for a term. The president, or should I say the counsellor, was like the modern-day mayor. They handled security matters among other things. So, if the city was in trouble, the counsellor would ring the cathedral bell, calling on all the guild representatives to form defence groups. Some people think this call to arms might be where the *somatén* a Catalan term for a citizen militia came from.

SOME INFO

Now, let me tell you a little something about the Consell de Cent. These were the guys in charge of the keys to the city walls. Just like those shopping centres in Britain, their crew would open the city gates at half-past five in the morning and close at six in the evening.

The Mediterranean, A Sea Under Catalan Law

Back in the day when Pere III of Aragon, also known as "the Great" 1240-1285, was in charge after his father Jaume I, he decided to build the Royal Shipyards of Barcelona, or *Reials Drassanes de Barcelona.* Around that time, he also set up the Consulate of the Sea, a legal body that governed maritime affairs in Catalan waters.

Standard of the House of Aragón.

❖ ❖ ❖

The Consulate of the Sea was made up of consuls appointed by the Consell de Cent. These consuls were chosen from honest citizens who had experience in business dealings, and they were like the urban aristocrats of their time. When it came to maritime matters, whether it was about cargo, damages, or lost goods, the Consulate had more authority than the regular justice system. Some cities with international ports recognized the importance of this institution to such an extent

Entrance of the Barcelona Shipyards.

> **About Vocabulary**
> According to Joan Corominas, the Catalan term *drassana* and the Spanish term *atarazana* have the same Arabic origin and mean "ship arsenal," "place where ships are built," or "manufacturing house." The earliest known document mentioning the Catalan term *drassana* dates back to 1245.

that its jurisdiction expanded to cover the most important points of the commercial maritime network in the Mediterranean.

The Book of The Consulate of The Sea

The son of this second Pere, Pere III the Ceremonious (1319-1387), turned the Consulate of the Sea into a Supreme Court. The court's regulations became established as case law, which was then compiled in the *Book of the Consulate of the Sea.* The volume became so prestigious overseas that many foreign governments asked for copies of the manuscript in exchange for a hefty sum of coins.

SOME INFO

Legend has it that Venice was one of the first cities allowed to copy the book. In gratitude, the Venetians gifted Barcelona a clock tower, which was supposedly the first ever installed in the city. This very clock would later be placed in the cathedral in 1393.

Many foreign governments asked for copies of the edition of the *Book of the Consulate of the Sea.*

The Generalitat: A Tax for the King's Benefit

Pere the Ceremonious wasn't just busy writing legal books about the sea. He also took the time to establish the Generalitat of Catalonia.

❖ ❖ ❖

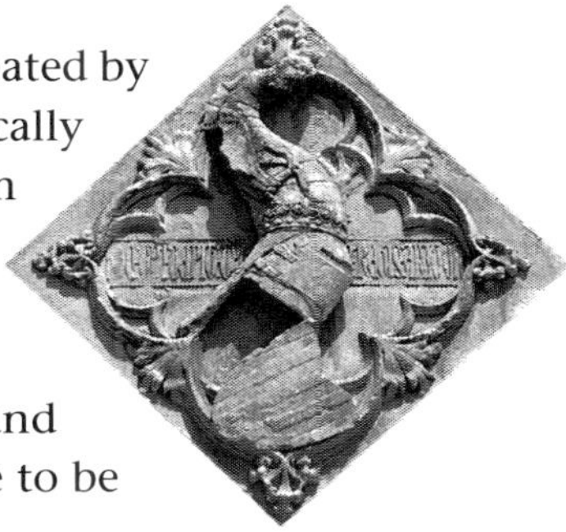

Coat of Arms of Pere III the Ceremonious.

The General's Deputation, which was created by the king in the 14th century, was basically a permanent group of representatives from Las Cortes whose main job was to collect taxes requested by the monarch from the powerful estates. They named this tax "Rights of the General" or "Generalities," and as time went on, the institution itself came to be known as the Generalitat.

Initially, this commission from Las Cortes operated on and off, but it eventually grew and became a permanent agency based in Barcelona for collecting taxes.

The Queen's Insomnia

Leonor of Sicily 1325-1375 was Pere the Ceremonious' third wife. She married her cousin when she was just fourteen years old and soon realized that it would be difficult for her to sleep in the palace walls. The constant noise from the daily market in the square made it clear to Leonor that she had no choice but to move to a different residence. The new place that allowed the queen to sleep peacefully was the former Temple House, a palace built on the southern side of the Roman wall, which the bishopric offered to the king in exchange for other lands. It's been many years since people could visit the Palau de la Reina or Palau Reial Menor, as it was demolished in the mid-19th century.

SOME INFO

The writer Bernat Metge, who was pretty close to King Joan I ended up getting locked up in the *Palau Reial Menor* for a while. Why, you ask? Well, they said he was involved in some shady business, supposedly taking commissions from who knows where.

Cloister of the Monastery of Santa Maria de Pedralbes.

A Monastery for a Lonely Queen

Jaume II the Just (1267-1327), brother of Pere the Ceremonious, and his wife Elisenda de Montcada (1292-1364), had this grand plan. They built this massive Gothic complex called the Royal Monastery of Santa Maria de Pedralbes in1326. Why? Because they thought Jaime was going to die soon, and Elisenda needed a new place to live.

Less than a year later, Elisenda only thirty-seven and recently widowed, found herself in that fancy new home. The place ended up becoming a home for Clarisse nuns, most of them from noble families. Elisenda had a hand in securing some royal privileges for the architectural complex, like being protected by the Consell de Cent, who promised to defend it if it was ever attacked. So, when the nuns got kicked out during the *Guerra dels Segadors* (Reaper's War), a group of soldiers, along with the city's second counsellor, made sure the religious women got safely to another place.

A Tomb Picked by Its Future Occupant

Queen Elisenda had her sepulchre built for herself while she was still alive and well! It's like a fancy mausoleum situated on the wall that divides the church and the cloister. On the side of the tomb facing the cloister, which is the area reserved for the nuns, the queen is depicted as a nun herself. But when you look at the part of the tomb inside the church, which is open to the public, she's all dressed up in her royal robes with a shiny crown on her head.

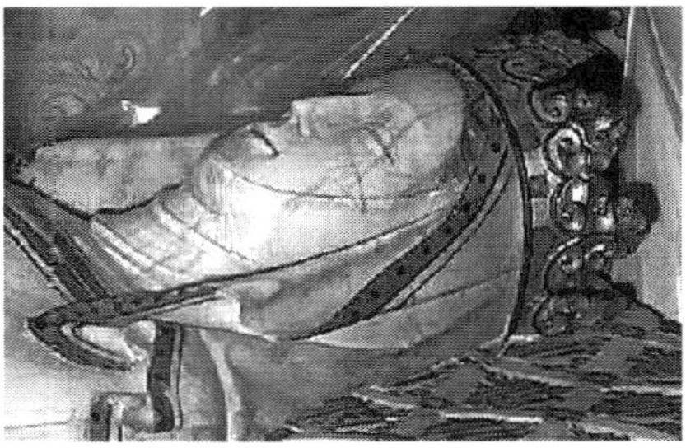

Queen Elisenda de Montcada's Mausoleum.

SOME INFO

The monastery is a pretty straightforward geometric structure, nothing too fancy. You'll see Queen Elisenda's coat of arms and the House of Barcelona's four bars proudly displayed on the main door. But the real standout is the cloister, which is three stories tall—quite unique, right? And there are still a few nuns living in the monastery to this day.

The Chemical Inventions of King Juan

Joan I, aka Joan the Hunter, was quite the character back in the day (1350-1396). He was known for his astrology skills, and it's rumoured he had this secret alchemy workshop set up in the basement of the Palau del Rei. What was he up to down there, you ask?

❖ ❖ ❖

Joan I, the Hunter.

Well, like all the other science geeks of that time, he was probably dabbling in all sorts of magical potions to make people fall head over heels for him. And he was also on a mission to find the ultimate cure for any ailment known to humanity. But the real jackpot he was after was the philosopher's stone, a legendary recipe for making gold right at home. Some people thought it involved mixing mercury and sulphur, while others believed it was some kind of mysterious gas. Who knows? But there are still people out there hunting for it to this day! By the way, this philosopher's stone business reminds me of something Hobbes once said: the only real philosopher's stone is the headstone in the cemetery. Deep stuff.

Did you know?
Joan I decided to copy this cool celebration that was happening in Toulouse, a city in Occitania. He started the Floral Games of Barcelona in 1393. Those Catalan-Aragonese rulers kept the tradition going until the late 15th century.

Death To Those Blamed for Causing the Black Death

So, back in 1391, just like in the Kingdom of Castile, people started persecuting the Jews in the major cities of Europe, including Barcelona. People blamed them for the Black Death that had devastated much of the continent. Death was the punishment they had in mind for many of them.

Burning of Jewish people blamed for causing the plague.

❖ ❖ ❖

The city was in deep crisis because of all this. The authorities in Barcelona tried to fix things by setting up a public bank called the *Taula de Canvi* (Table of Exchange) in 1401. The idea was to make up for the vacuum left by the disappearance of the Jews to boost the social and economic situation. But this didn't fix a thing. The city was already going down the drain.

The Vacuum Left in the Afflicted City

After the Black Death in 1348, Barcelona lost half of its population. Not everyone died, though. Many people decided to flee to the countryside to get away from the disease. With such a grim future ahead, the streets were filled with doomsday preachers screaming to the heavens, demanding justice for the epidemic. People also came up with some wild remedies to try and prevent the bubonic plague: throwing salt on their doorsteps, pouring vinegar on the ground, downing Greek wine, lighting fires with fancy-smelling plants, burning orange and lemon peels, and more. They were desperate to try anything to avoid that plague. The plague made a comeback, though, with less intensity, in 1362 and 1371. To add to the bad harvests because of droughts they'd suffered since 1331 they now had abandoned crops. The consequences of what they called "The first bad year" hung around for a long time.

King Martí's Viewpoint from the *Plaça del Rei*.

The Tallest Building in The World Was in Barcelona

So, there's this building called Mirador del Rey Martí (King Martin's Viewpoint), part of the Palau Reial Major architectural complex. It's a five-story tower nestled between Palau del Lloctinent and Salón del Tinell aka Tinell Hall .

❖ ❖ ❖

Legend has it that it was named after Martí the Humane (1356-1410), who became king after his brother Juan I passed away without any heirs. Apparently, people thought Martí had this huge tower constructed at the very spot where the viewpoint stands today.

But here's the thing: that tower had nothing to do with Martí. The timing doesn't add up since he died in 1410 and the tower wasn't built until 1555.

The people of Barcelona used to boast to foreigners that this tower was the tallest in the whole world. But they weren't just pulling legs. Many of them genuinely believed it!

The Generalitat Gains Momentum

During the time when King Martí the Humane was on the throne, something interesting happened—the acquisition of the house that would later become the core of the Palau de la Generalitat.

❖ ❖ ❖

King Martí the Humane and his son Martí the Younger during the transfer of the remains of Sant Sever in Barcelona in 1405.

This house was located on Sant Honorat Street and was bought by representatives of the three estates of the Courts back in 1400. They paid 38,500 sueldos for it.

Now, when the king passed away, the Catalan General Council decided to establish a temporary government with a parliament that lasted for a couple of years. The Cortes of 1413 played a significant role in reorganizing the Generalitat, giving it a political character. This was a crucial step towards the growth of the institution and its self-governance.

SOME INFO

The *Palau de la Generalitat* is a building which is architecturally highly heterogeneous, as it grew while new plots of land were acquired and additions from nearby properties were made.

Did you know?
The façade, which is still standing today, was built between 1597 and 1602. It was the first in the city to be built in the Renaissance style, and its creation was the work of the architect Pere Blai (1553-1620).

Tough Times for A Palace with an Illustrious Past

The Palau de la Generalitat used to be home to a Catalan government that operated independently from the central authority. This lasted until September 11th, 1714, when Felipe V took control of Barcelona. Since then, a significant stretch of history had to pass before the Generalitat once again found its place within the building.

In 1931, Francesc Macià restored the institution's power after the Spanish municipal elections. Lluís Companys continued in his footsteps, but Franco arrived and held onto power for many years. It wasn't until September 1977, almost two years after the dictator's death, that the Generalitat was officially reinstated.

SOME INFO

The *Palau de la Generalitat* is among the few medieval buildings in Europe that still serve as the headquarters for the institution it was built for.

Did you know?
A staggering 129 presidents have presided over this building since its inception to the present day.

Facade of the *Palau de la Generalitat.*

From Compromise to Imposition: A New Dynasty Comes into Play

So, Martí the Humane breathed his last, bringing an end to an era that started way back with Guifred the Hairy and House of Barcelona. Now that the late king was no more, it was time to figure out who would take the reins of the three states he left behind.

❖ ❖ ❖

Coronation of Ferran of Antequera, grandson of Pere the Ceremonious.

That's when the Compromise of Casp took place between 1410 and 1412, a big gathering that brought together representatives from Aragon, Valencia, and Catalonia. They were there to decide on Martí's successor.

You'd think there would be some serious deliberation with multiple candidates, but in reality, the decision was pretty much a done deal beforehand, thanks to Pope Luna's influence. The chosen one was Ferran of Antequera (1380-1416), a Castilian who happened to be Peter the Ceremonicus' grandson and part of the Trastámara family.

Once this election took place, the leaders of the institutions in Barcelona started to get seriously worried. They were used to dealing with the Catalan-Aragonese crown's compromising ways, but things took a sharp turn with the Castilian kings in power. They were dead set on calling all the shots and weren't about to give in to the powerful factions in the city.

When Barcelona Split in Two

When Barcelona was going through some rough times under Alfons the Magnanimous's rule (1396-1458), things got pretty tense. The economy was in a sorry state, and the Generalitat and the Consell de Cent decided to put in place a bunch of protectionist measures that didn't sit well with the wealthy city elite.

❖ ❖ ❖

Alfons the Magnanimous, King of Aragon, Valencia, Mallorca, Sicily, Sardinia, and Naples, and Count of Barcelona. Painting by the Valencian painter Joan de Joanes.

As things got worse, the people of Barcelona split into two groups. On one side, you had the reformist party called *la Busca*, made up of craftsmen, artisans, some lower-ranking nobles, and a few not-so-wealthy merchants. They were fighting for equality and wanted to shake things up. On the other side, you had the Barcelona oligarchy forming a party called *la Biga* to defend their privileges and keep things as they were.

Then, in 1453, the governor and lieutenant general of Catalonia, Galcerà of Requesens (?-1465), made a move that would be considered a full-blown coup nowadays. He suspended the elections to replace members of the Barcelona Council and handed over the city's power to la Busca.

La Busca wasted no time in making changes. They tinkered with the Consell de Cent by adding five advisors to the decision-making body: two honest citizens, a merchant, an artist, and an artisan. It was a big deal because, for the first time, the lower classes had a say in the power structure. They also trimmed down the number of positions to prevent excessive bureaucracy and lowered salaries in an attempt to recover from the mess.

Joan II of Aragon took the side of the citizens who belonged to *La Biga*, which represented the most powerful, to the detriment of *La Busca*, who were merchants and craftsmen. Painting by Manuel Aguirre and Monsalbe 1885. Below, coat of arms of the Casal dynasty of Barcelona.

So, Barcelona was pretty divided back then, with *la Busca* fighting for a fairer system and *la Biga* trying to protect their own interests.

La Biga launched a counterattack, considering that the coup had been quite half-hearted, and the Generalitat had offered continuous support to the most powerful. The lower ranks saw their hopes frustrated. In 1462, the Catalan Civil War broke out and *la Busca* lost power, which fell back into the hands of the rich and powerful.

Did you know?

The Catalan Civil War (1462-1472) broke out because of the clash between the Catalan-Aragonese compromise approach and the heavy-handed Trastámara rulers. However, this whole crisis brought a fresh battle to the already chaotic century: the first remensa war remensa being the cash that poor peasants had to cough up to their lords to abandon their land. The peasants got all fired up and rose up to demand an end to the oppression they had to deal with from the rich landowners.

Commemorative sculpture of the 500th anniversary of the remensa compromise by royal arbitration, signed in the monastery of Amer in 1485.

The Peasant Who Tried to Kill Ferran II

It was a Friday in December, 1492, just two months after Columbus set foot on American shores, when something quite dramatic unfolded in Barcelona. Ferdinand II the Catholic, a reigning monarch, was leisurely leaving the Santa Àgata chapel in the company of his wife, Isabella of Castile. Out of nowhere, a man armed with a sword suddenly appeared and launched an attack on the royal couple.

❖ ❖ ❖

Ferran II was attacked and wounded on the stairs of the *Plaça del Rei* in Barcelona.

Fortunately, Ferran's guards swiftly intervened, managing to apprehend the assailant in the nick of time. Nonetheless, the crazed man did manage to graze the king's neck with his weapon. The individual responsible for this shocking incident was none other than Joan de Canyamars, a peasant regarded by some as mentally unstable and by others as a staunch advocate for land rights.

In order to send a clear message about the dire consequences of attempting to harm the king, Ferdinand decreed a punishment that reeked of utmost cruelty and sadism. Canyamars was stripped bare and paraded around the city atop a cart. At each square they passed, a portion of his body was mercilessly torn away—his eyes, his nipples, his limbs, and so on. As the day neared its end, he was subjected to a stoning, and eventually, both he and the cart were set ablaze.

SOME INFO

According to Joan Amades, some people claim that you can still spot three drops of blood on the third step of the staircase in the Santa Àgata Chapel. Supposedly, they're from Ferran II's neck. Are they really there?

Did you know?
When Ferran and Isabel tied the knot, it was like a symbolic bond between the Kingdom of Castile and the Crown of Aragon. This union made the monarchs even more powerful. But their marriage also marked the end of the Trastámara dynasty. Their daughter, Juana I of Castile (1479-1555), also known as Juana the Mad, got married to Felipe the Handsome (1478-1506). Together, they had a boy named Carlos I of Spain and V of Germany (1500-1558). He's the one who kicked off the Habsburg dynasty.

The Catholic monarchs, Ferran and Isabel's marriage above, ended the Trastámara dynasty. Their daughter Juana I married Felipe the Handsome below.

The Terror of The Inquisition Reaches Barcelona

Ferran the Catholic isn't just known for one specific atrocity. This king holds the rather infamous distinction of being the ruler who established the Inquisition tribunal in Spain. He wanted to tackle the issue of Jews with a "definitive method," so he borrowed the approach created by the Roman Pontiff Gregory IX back in 1231 to root out heresies.

❖ ❖ ❖

The tribunal of the Inquisition, promoted by King Ferran the Catholic, was a "definitive method" to eradicate heretics.

In 1542, in Barcelona, the Holy Inquisition tribunal was set up in one of the buildings attached to the Palau del Rei, which is now the Frederic Marès Museum located on Dels Comtes Street. During the reign of Felipe II of Castile (1527-1598), the son of Carlos I of Spain, this Renaissance palace witnessed horrifying torture practices. Among the devices used in these buildings was the Iron Maiden, a metal enclosure tall enough to trap a person inside.

Through a small door, the victim would be forced to enter. Once inside, they would be surrounded by sharp objects, restricting their movement while being interrogated. If, after the questioning, the inquisitors considered the tortured individual to be an unrepentant heretic who refused to convert to Christianity, they could sentence them to death by burning them at the stake.

SOME INFO

On one of the external walls of the building, you can still see the polychrome shield representing the Holy Office of the Inquisition.

Did you know?
If you look closely at the walls, you can spot some scribbles in Hebrew. It seems like they built the place after destroying the Jewish quarter and reusing some of the stones.

The Birth of a 'Bastard' Child: Censorship

Felipe II.

Now, let's talk about Felipe II. He decided to take some drastic steps to prevent any trouble caused by the Protestant Reformation that was happening in Europe. Starting in 1568, he banned the people of Barcelona from going to foreign universities. And if that wasn't enough, he wouldn't let French ecclesiastics teach in the city either.

Catholic Castile, always suspicious of Barcelona's feisty nature, was afraid that the city would catch some heretical ideas from those Lutheran and Huguenot Europeans. So, they not only fortified the borders but also decided to bring in censorship.

That's when the shadow of the scissors started creeping into the picture, threatening all the books published in Barcelona.

Did you know?
In 1834, the Inquisition disappeared in the peninsula by decree of the regent María Cristina de Borbón-Dos Sicilias (1806-1878).

When an Anthem Was Born out of War

Between 1640 and 1652, the Catalans found themselves caught up in a brutal war with the central power. There were several reasons for this. In Barcelona, tensions escalated among the ruling classes due to the Madrid government's centralizing tendencies. Not only did this endanger their institutions, but it also threatened the privileges they had enjoyed since the Late Middle Ages.

❖ ❖ ❖

Portrait painted by Velázquez of the Count-Duke of Olivares.

At the same time, the peasants grew tired of being victims of the oppressive seigneurial regime imposed by both Madrid and Barcelona. As if that wasn't enough, the lower middle class helplessly witnessed an increase in taxes as a result of the kingdom's capital city's demands. Meanwhile, in Madrid, the influential Count-Duke of Olivares (1587-1645) became increasingly frustrated with the fact that Catalan laws didn't favour the monarchy as much as those of Castile. It was this difference in laws that sparked the revolt.

A Very Bloody Corpus Christi Day

Felipe IV's (1605-1665) army was marching towards France to take part in the Thirty Years' War (1618-1648), and they had to pass through Catalonia to reach French-speaking lands. According to Catalan laws, the people were required to provide the army with salt, vinegar, water, and a bed.

However, the ten thousand men who made up Felipe's troops didn't think that this basic provision was enough, and they began to abuse the population in various ways.

The uprising of the peasants on Corpus Christi Day in 1640.

After months filled with fights, persecutions, and some frustrated attempts to reach agreements, on June 7, 1640, Corpus Christi Day, a wave of pent-up anger erupted into a violent peasant uprising that engulfed the city. This event, now known as the Day of the Corpus of Blood, has left an indelible mark on history.

The Drop That Started the War Of The Reapers

Statue of Pau Claris, by Rafael Atché.

It was Corpus Christi Day, and the Viceroy of Catalonia, Dalmau de Queralt (1638-1640), died under uncertain circumstances on the beach of Barcelona, in front of Montjuïc. Some authors claim that the man had suffered a fatal fall from his horse and that, once on the ground lifeless, the people in the street stabbed him. Others believe that Dalmau was directly assassinated. Whether death by accident or violence, Felip's army found this event the perfect excuse to attack the city.

The Generalitat and the *Consell de Cent* decided to defend Catalonia from the Castilian assault, and the President of the *Generalitat*, Pau Claris (1586-1641), went on to proclaim the Catalan Republic backed by institutions and the people. However, after a year-long siege and the onset of a devastating plague, Barcelona succumbed to foreign forces in 1652. In defeat, Catalonia once more acknowledged Castile as its ruler.

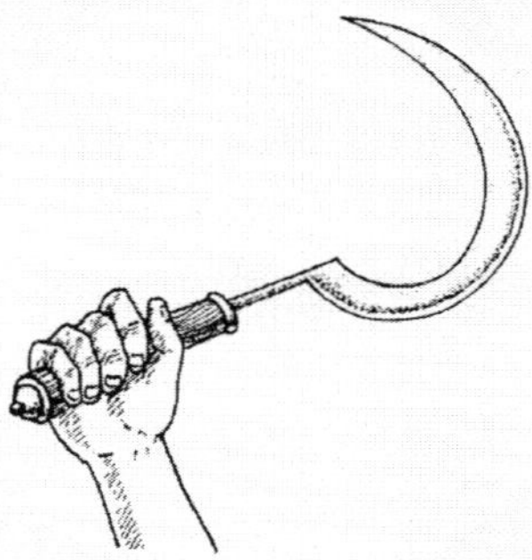

Did you know?
When the Reapers War and the plague epidemic hit Barcelona around 1650, it was a total disaster. The city was under siege, and the consequences were devastating. Roughly 15% to 20% of the population lost their lives during that period. It was a dark and tragic time for the people of Barcelona.

Bon cop de falç - A good strike of the sickle

Out of this unfortunate and sorrowful event that had a painful conclusion, the national anthem of Catalonia, *Els Segadors* (The Reapers), was born. The origins of the chant can be traced back to various songs that were popular during the time and circulated among the people until the 19th century.

Sheet music of *Els Segadors*, with the lyrics by Emili Guanyavents that have been preserved to this day.

In 1892, the melody was officially published for the first time, along with a musical and literary adaptation by Francesc Alió (1862-1908), a composer from Barcelona. The song was lengthy and included the most well-known refrains and verses. Then, in 1899, during the cultural movement known as *La Renaixença,* the political group *Union Catalanista* organized a competition to find the lyrics that best represented Catalonia's nationalist aspirations. The winning text, titled *Els Segadors,* was written by the poet and translator Emili Guanyavents (1860-1941). These lyrics are the ones that have lasted to this day.

Montjuïc Castle: A Fortress of Horrors

Back in the 16th century, Barcelona had quite easy access to the sea, despite being surrounded by walls. Those in charge didn't really think much about defence when they built the third fortified enclosure. But then trouble came knocking, and they had to reinforce the walls between 1521 and 1640 to avoid unnecessary headaches.

❖ ❖ ❖

Fast forward to 1640, during the rebellion against Felipe IV, and the construction of Montjuïc Castle began. They whipped up this protective structure, sitting over 170 meters above sea level, in just thirty days. They used two common materials found in the area: stone and mud. The place came in handy for military purposes after that, but it didn't become a proper castle until 1694. Now, the castle you see today isn't exactly how it used to be. It was wrecked and rebuilt lots of times. It even witnessed some gruesome events like torture and executions such as Francesc Ferrer i Guàrdia and Lluís Companys. If those walls could talk, you'd probably want to stick your fingers in your ears to avoid hearing anything!

Did you know?
In 1691, bombs indiscriminately launched from Montjuïc destroyed over a hundred houses in Barcelona. There were around 30,000 people living in the city at the time.

Montjuïc Castle today.

Felipe V Arrives: Barcelona Takes a Step Back

Portrait of Felipe V, by Jean Ranc 1723.

Felipe IV's son, Carlos II of Spain (1661-1700), turned out to be the last king of the House of Austria because he didn't have any heirs when he died in 1700. And you know what happened next? The War of the Spanish Succession kicked off!

❖ ❖ ❖

The fight was between the Bourbon dynasty, backing Felipe V of Castile (1683-1746), and the Habsburgs, who supported Archduke Carlos (1685-1740). But it wasn't just a family feud. The whole of Europe was holding its breath to see who would come out on top. Now, Barcelona was rooting for the archduke because they knew he wouldn't centralise power like Felipe V. On the other hand, those in the Kingdom of Castile, used to having authoritarian kings, didn't mind having a Bourbon ruler.

The Machinations of The War of The Spanish Succession

Archduke Carlos.

Right from the start, the War of the Spanish Succession was a big deal in terms of international politics. Louis XIV had imposed absolutism over in France, and some European dignitaries were worried that if Felipe V, who happened to be the grandson of the French king, came out on top in Spain, there might come a time when those two kingdoms would merge into one. Something they definitively didn't want. So, to stop any European royal family from getting too powerful,

French troops during the War of Succession.

England, the Netherlands, and Austria met up in Genoa in 1705 and had some secret talks with the Generalitat. They wanted to sign a pact backing Archduke Carlos. When they signed the Genoa Pact, it made the split between the Generalitat and Felipe V official. In August, the agreement's signatories arrived on the principality's coasts with significant firepower: three hundred ships and seventeen thousand soldiers. Felipe V's men, despite having the help of the French army, surrendered when faced with such a show of strength.

The European allies managed to reach Madrid but eventually withdrew because Felipe had the support of the people, making it difficult to maintain the occupation. France remained unwavering in its determination and focused all its energy on the campaign. Gradually, Felipe V regained control of the territories of the Crown of Aragon, one by one. Meanwhile, at the European level, the situation took a complete turn when Emperor Joseph I of Austria, Carlos' brother, suddenly passed away in 1711. Carlos had to replace him, which prompted a change in tactics for the allied countries. Now, just as Felipe V had been expanding his empire, Carlos found himself in the same position.

Considering the new circumstances, the major European powers reached an agreement with Louis XIV: no descendant of Felipe V could become the king of France. This pact brought an end to the international conflict, but the struggle of the Crown of Aragon against Felipe continued fiercely. England and Holland withdrew their support for the archduke, and Barcelona, one of the few places still holding out against Felipe V, became more isolated than ever before.

NUEVA PLANTA
DE LA
REAL AUDIENCIA
DEL PRINCIPADO
CATALUÑA,
ESTABLECIDA
POR SU MAGESTAD,
Con Decreto de Diez y [illegible] de Enero de mil setecientos diez y seis.

En Barcelona: Por Joseph Texido, Impresor del Rey Nuestro Señor.

Y Reimpreso en Gerona: Por Jofeph Bró, Impresor del Rey Nueftro Señor.

Manuscript of the Nueva Planta Decree issued by Felipe V, which had such disastrous consequences for Catalonia.

In July 1713, Felipe's troops launched a brutal siege of Barcelona, bombarding the city relentlessly. Despite being isolated, the city fought back with all its strength, but eventually had to surrender on September 11, 1714.

To ensure control over the newly conquered territory, they set up a Royal Superior Board of Justice and Government. The Generalitat, the Cortes, and the Consell de Cent were dissolved, and the people were disarmed. This marked the beginning of a severe crackdown on Catalonia's independence and its separation from the political landscape. As an act of humiliation, the executioner burned the documents of the Consell de Cent in public. The bishops of Vic, Tarragona, and Solsona were removed from their positions, and books published during the conflict were confiscated. All universities were shut down, and a new one was established in Cervera.

To complete their mission, they created the Nueva Planta Decree on January 16, 1716, which restructured the judicial and administrative system of the Principality. They implemented new fiscal laws and regulations to maintain control over the local municipalities. As a result, Catalonia lost its own governing institutions and could no longer govern itself.

Did you know?

More than 40,000 people from Barcelona sadly lost their lives during the siege. A lot of them were laid to rest at the *Fossar de les Moreres*, a spot where they now honour those who fell in that war.

La Ciutadella: Felipe V's Military Fortress

If Montjuïc Castle was built to keep Felipe IV's troops in check, then *La Ciutadella* (The Citadel) was commissioned by Felipe V himself. The king had no second thoughts about tearing down a part of the Ribera neighbourhood to erect this fortress, all in an effort to keep Catalonia under control. And so, the number of soldiers stationed in Catalan territory never fell below twenty thousand.

The former Royal Palace of La Ciutadella is now the headquarters of the Parliament of Catalonia.

❖ ❖ ❖

Today, only the main internal structures of the fortress remain intact. These include the *Palau del Gobernador*, which now houses an institute, the chapel, and the arsenal. The arsenal, originally used for storing gunpowder and bullets, was transformed into the *Palau Reial* in 1888. In 1931, and again in 1979, after the end of the Franco dictatorship, it was chosen as the location for the Parliament of Catalonia.

About Vocabulary
The streets of Villarroel and Casanova have something in common: they are both named after Catalans who fought against the troops of Felipe V. Antoni de Villarroel (1656-1726) fought as a military officer, while Rafael Casanova (1660-1743) was serving as a Councillor of Barcelona.

SOME INFO

At the time of its construction, La Ciutadella was the largest citadel in Europe, boasting a star-shaped design. The former Palau Reial of La Ciutadella now houses the Parliament of Catalonia.

Did you know?
In Ciutadella Park, you'll find a statue of General Joan Prim from Reus (1814-1870). It was Prim who, aware of the city's wishes, decreed the transfer of the fortress to Barcelona in 1868 during his tenure as head of the Spanish government. The demolition of La Ciutadella would continue until 1878.

Three Martyrs from Barcelona Against Napoleon

We all know that Napoleon Bonaparte (1769-1821) had grand ambitions of conquering the world. It's also common knowledge that his troops, using the excuse of occupying Portugal, decided to stay in Spain and conquer the Spanish lands as well.

❖ ❖ ❖

The sculptural ensemble by Josep Llimona dedicated to the martyrs against Napoleon is in Garriga i Bachs Square.

The presence of French soldiers in Barcelona certainly irritated the locals, but only a few dared to stand up against the soldiers who took advantage of their position. Hoping that the people would join their rebellion, a group of dissenters initiated what history now remembers as the May 1809 Conspiracy. Unfortunately, the uprising didn't yield the expected results, and the instigators paid a heavy price when they were executed by the French troops shortly after. On May 11, 1809, as five of the insurgents faced exemplary punishment in the Ciutadella, three courageous individuals sought to make their voices heard. Julià Poblet, Ramon Mas, and Pere Les Torres, residents of Barcelona, decided to ring the cathedral bells to rally the people against the French invaders. However, their act of defiance cost them their lives, as they were also executed.

Did you know?

The bronze sculpture by Josep Llimona, titled *Monument to the Heroes of 1809*, depicts the attempted revolt orchestrated by these men. You can find this sculpture in Garriga i Bachs Square, capturing the final moments of the first five insurgents before they met their deaths by garrotte.

The Widest Street in Barcelona

For several years, the city's authorities had been mulling over the idea of making Barcelona larger and more efficient. And so, in 1824, *Passeig de Gràcia* was born.

❖ ❖ ❖

Their goal was to create a grand boulevard with a broad and smooth pavement that would make it easier for carriages and horses to get around. They decided to follow the path of the old *Camino de Jesús,* which connected Barcelona with Gràcia. Back then, this road was bordered by vegetable gardens and country houses. Little did they know that this initial idea would help rise one of the most famous and bustling streets in all of Europe.

Passeig de Gràcia at the end of the 19th century and the end of the 20th century.

Passeig de Gràcia quickly became the heart of the new Barcelona, and over time, both sides of the avenue became populated. This marked the birth of what we now call the Left and Right of the *Eixample,* two distinct neighbourhoods with their own distinct characteristics. The Catalan bourgeoisie, who were initially sceptical of the project, wasted no time in claiming the "the front rows" in this modern and fashionable area.

Did you know?
Passeig de Gràcia is a whopping forty-two meters wide, making it the widest street in the entire city. It's not surprising that it became the favoured spot for leisurely strolls among the Catalan bourgeoisie.

A Bad Bull and Half the City in Flames

The Salic Law, which was a part of Spanish jurisprudence, meant that women couldn't sit on the throne. In order to prepare for the future, Ferdinand VII (1784-1833), who had only two daughters, decided to get rid of this rule by passing the Pragmatic Sanction. But Ferdinand's brother, Carlos María Isidro (1788-1855), who believed he should be the king instead with so many nieces around, didn't agree with these changes.

❖ ❖ ❖

With the help of the Church, he started a war to seize power, using the slogan God, Fatherland, Charters, and King. The Carlists were against the *Isabelinos*, who supported Ferdinand's daughter, the future Isabel II (1830-1904). She was just three years old when the disputes began.

Against this backdrop of conflict, Reus became the starting point for a series of events called *bullangas*, which would pop up again in different Catalan cities in the coming years. On July 22, 1835, after a group of Carlists killed some liberal prisoners, there was a lot of anger, and two convents were set on fire in Reus, resulting in the death of four religious' devotees. Soon, the fury spread to Barcelona. Just four days later, after a terrible bullfight at the Barceloneta bullring, the city was engulfed in flames. The audience was disappointed by the bullfight, and they started throwing benches and objects into the arena. Someone even dragged a dying bull from the bullring to La Rambla. The agitators multiplied, delivering impassioned speeches against the clergy and enemies of liberalism. The tension escalated to the point where major convents in the city were set on fire, and several religious devotees were killed.

The troops and the protesters, in front of the Holy Cross Theatre, during the *bullanga* of May 4, 1837 anonymous engraving.

Barcelona Grows on Top of Its Convents

After the fire, the so-called *desamortización* ecclesiastical confiscations de Mendizábal fell upon the convents in Barcelona, following the laws of 1836 and 1837. Juan Álvarez Mendizábal (1790-1853) had become the Minister of Finance in Spain in 1835. He was chosen by José María Queipo de Llano (1786-1843), one of the regents of the young Queen Isabel II.

❖ ❖ ❖

Juan Álvarez Mendizábal.

Mendizábal had a strong reputation as a liberal, which made him a suitable candidate for the monarchy at the time. The *desamortización* involved the complete seizure of the Church's properties and selling them through auctions to raise funds for the government. The goal was to utilize unproductive assets to boost agriculture and create economically active areas in cities. The aim was to encourage a greater circulation of money and establish a middle class capable of driving economic growth. Unfortunately, Mendizábal was dismissed from his position and couldn't complete the task he had initiated.

Within a short period, 80% of the Church's possessions inside the walled enclosure of Barcelona were auctioned off. As a result of these confiscations, the city experienced an unprecedented wave of urbanization. The buyers of the monasteries and convents promptly demolished them to construct private buildings and public spaces.

José María Queipo de Llano.

The Most Spectacular Expansion of the City

The most long-awaited demolition: "Down with the walls!"

The medieval wall of *las Drassanes* the shipyards.

For centuries, Barcelona's growth was hindered due to military reasons. Building in the Plain of Barcelona was strictly forbidden to ensure that the city had enough space to safely launch cannon shots without endangering its own people. The protective walls marked the limit, and if we trace the trajectory of the imaginary cannonball, it would lead us to the present location of the *Jardinets de Gracia* Gracia's (Little Gardens), where *Passeig de Gracia* ends at its upper part.

However, this ban was killing Barcelona. The city was becoming overcrowded, and space was becoming scarce. Life within the walls during the 18th and early 19th centuries was tough to endure. The affluent individuals had an average lifespan of 36 years, while the poor were lucky to make it to 23. What's more, there was a lack of basic public services like sewage and running water. The city was plagued by epidemics, pollution, and filth, which posed a serious threat to its survival. In 1841, a book titled *Down with the Walls* by Dr. Pere Felip Monlau (1808-1871), a hygienist, was published, sparking a fervent demand for change in Barcelona. The city desperately needed more open space and fewer solid barriers.

Despite the citizen mobilization, with people rallying behind the slogan "Down with the walls," it took over ten years for the central government to finally take action. Thanks to the efforts of a Catalan minister, Barcelona's plea for expansion was even-

Did you know?
There aren't as many medieval wall remnants compared to the Roman ones. If you want to check out what's left of Barcelona's third wall, you have to head over to Paral·lel, specifically the Santa Madrona or *Drassanes* gate. This part is the only piece that managed to survive after the rest got torn down in the 19th century.

tually accepted opening the city. They gave the go ahead to tear down all the walls except the one that looks out to the sea. They wanted to keep Montjuïc Castle and the Ciutadella too. They were still worried about possible attacks.

After the Walls, Growth

After spending so many years 'walled in', it was time to figure out how the new city should look. So, back in 1859, the Barcelona City Council decided to hold a competition to find the best project for the city's grand expansion.

Thirteen different projects were submitted, but the one by architect Antoni Rovira i Trias (1816-1889) was the chosen winner. However, the Spanish government had its own plan and forced it upon the city through a royal decree. It was a plan by Ildefons Cerdà (1815-1876), who was working as an engineer at the State Public Works Prefecture at that time.

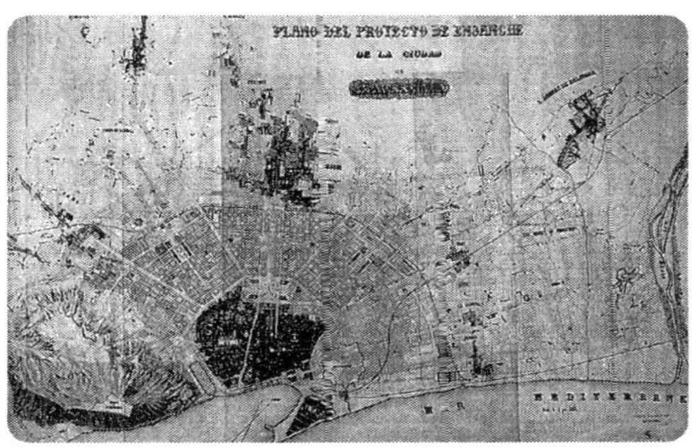

The project presented by Antoni Rovira i Trias.

This didn't sit well with the City Council, leading to tension between them and the central State. It was no surprise that political manoeuvring became the norm, causing frustrating delays in the construction process.

A Visionary Modernizes Barcelona

The Cerdà Plan was totally groundbreaking! It was all about being smart, practical, and forward-thinking when it came to designing a city. Back then, people were used to cities that were very different from his ideas. But Cerdà? He had big dreams. He envisioned a city like no other, and he wasn't afraid to shake things up.

If you took a close look at the cities of that era, you'd realize just how different Cerdà's ideas were. He didn't accept the whole "space is a privilege" idea that everyone else accepted. He had grand plans for a future where everyone could enjoy a life of happiness and comfort. He was a real trailblazer.

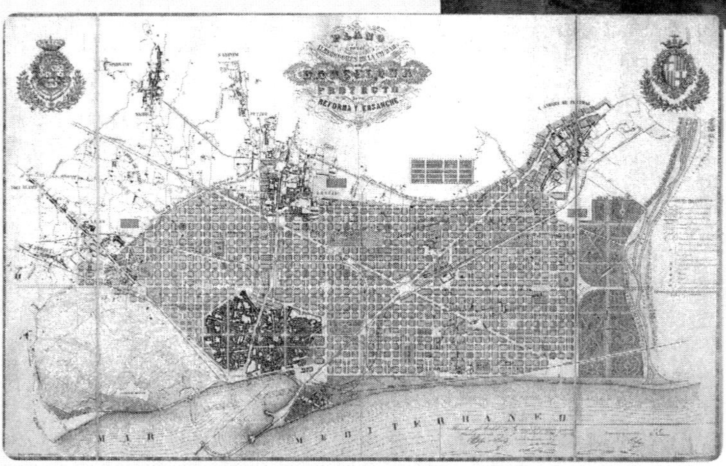

Some of the Main Characteristics of the Cerdà Plan

Cerdà had this grand idea of creating a city that would make its residents feel physically and mentally great. So, he came up with some basic plans for the project, for example:

❖ The Eixample would be divided into blocks that were 113.3 meters on each side, and the corners would be cut at an angle, giving them a sort of octagon shape. This geometric shape made it easier for carriages to move around and see everything clearly.

❖ The streets were nice and wide, at least twenty metres in width. They were divided into a ten-metre road in the middle and two five-hundred-centimetre pavements on either side. These spacious streets were designed to provide comfort for the people of Barcelona, allowing them to walk without any worries.

❖ The buildings were planned with proper spacing, and their height couldn't be taller than the width of the streets. This ensured that all residents would receive sunlight in their homes.

❖ Every house was required to have windows on both the front and back to allow for good ventilation.

❖ It was important to create spaces for children and the elderly, which is why the idea of having gardens inside the city blocks was introduced.

With the implementation of the Cerdà Plan, Barcelona became a modern city with numerous public services. Considering the previous plagues and epidemics that had affected the city, collective sanitation and hygiene measures were high on their agenda. This resulted in the construction of fountains, public washing areas, public baths, and large sewer systems.

Other services and facilities were also established, such as gas lamps, and horse-drawn carriages available for public rental with fixed stops on streets and squares. Additionally, thanks to the efforts of Rovira and Trias, a fire department was set up. Interurban postal service, municipal slaughterhouses, and cemeteries were also established during this time. Later, the telegraph, public electric lighting, and the first telephones were introduced.

Did you know?
With his *Teoría general de la urbanización* (General Theory of Urbanisation) Ildefons Cerdà became known as one of the founders of modern urbanism.

Some projects were owned by the public, while others were made possible through private initiatives. Despite initial resistance, investors saw the potential profitability of the expansion, and citizens became enthusiastic about the idea of a new Barcelona.

SOME INFO

Cerdà ended up in financial ruin because both the Spanish State and the Barcelona City Council owed him money.

The People from *Can Fanga* Turn Up

When they started building the Eixample, the streets and sidewalks were not paved. The rains, sometimes heavy, turned the neighbourhood into a huge mud puddle, and carriages and horses accidentally splashed pedestrians. To keep the mud from getting inside the houses, they installed a rectangular iron piece at the entrance of the buildings. People could use it to clean their shoes before entering. You can still find some of these contraptions in some old houses in the *Eixample*. Because of all the accumulated mud, the people of Barcelona became known as *Los de Can Fanga* (The muddy ones) from the city.

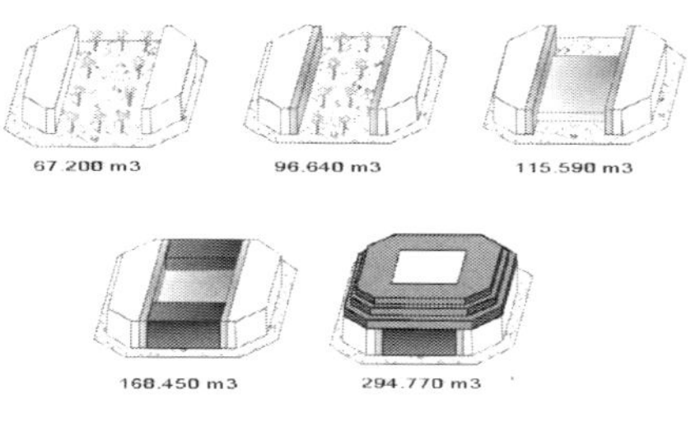

The original plan was changed to create more living space and make more money.

Made the Law, Created a Thousand Tricks

Some of the measures in the Cerdà Plan for the well-being of the citizens didn't last long. Crafty builders found a clever way to bypass the regulation of four floors per building. They didn't count the ground floors because those were meant for businesses. According to their reasoning, the first floor always came after the mezzanine and the main floor. With this excuse, which the City Council accepted, buildings ended up having seven floors. This trick was just one of many. Right from the beginning, many of the interior gardens disappeared as warehouses, storage spaces, and secondary buildings were constructed, mainly for businesses.

Classic interior of an Eixample block, according to the original idea of leaving a landscaped space.

Money Goes Up in a Lift

In the Eixample neighbourhood, the residents of buildings had a certain social hierarchy. The wealthier individuals typically lived on the main floor, while the caretaker and offices were situated on the top floor or mezzanine. Other flats were bought or rented by neighbours based on their financial means.

In the past, before lifts were installed in private buildings, the price of a home went down as one climbed the stairs. This clearly indicated that someone living on the fourth floor had less money compared to someone on the second floor. However, with the advent of lifts, the value of flats started to become less distinguishable. Eventually, with the construction of penthouses and flats on the rooftop, the price structure was completely flipped.
Now, the wealthier social classes chose to take the lift to the higher floors.

Did you know?
The Cerdà Plan aimed to connect Barcelona with the surrounding towns. In 1897, the Aggregation Act was approved, incorporating Vila de Gràcia, Sant Gervasi de Cassoles, Les Corts de Sarrià, Sants, Sant Andreu de Palomar, and Sant Martí de Provençals.

SOME INFO

Cerdà's project played a significant role in the growth of the city's industry and contributed to Barcelona's rise as one of the leading cities in the country by the turn of the century.

The Most Festive Street in Barcelona

El Paral·lel, synonymous with party and spectacle.

Until the 1970s, Avenida del Paral·lel (Parallel Avenue) was the ultimate street for theatres, bars, and music halls in Barcelona. It was the go-to place for fun, drinks, and mischief, boasting theatres and three music halls.

❖ ❖ ❖

Even if people were short of cash, everyone, regardless of age or status, would take a stroll on Paral·lel. It was one of the rare streets where you could party all night long, and the people themselves were the main attraction. The avenue's development started in the 1830s when some of Barcelona's industries were established outside the city walls. They needed a less crowded route for carts transporting materials. That's how this wide road came into existence, running alongside the walls from Portal de Santa Madrona to the end of Sant Pau Street. Soon enough, working-class neighbourhoods sprouted up along the margins of this road, due to the proximity to the industries. According to historical records, the decision to name the avenue Paral·lel was made because its layout coincided with a terrestrial parallel: the 41° 22′ 34″ north. It's believed that Ildefons Cerdà, aware of this fact, chose the name. With its established identity, neighbours, and traffic, the wide circular road transformed into an avenue under the "General Plan of the Expansion of Barcelona" and was officially inaugurated in 1894.

Barcelona Shows Off to the World: The Universal Exhibition of 1888

❖ ❖ ❖

A venue worthy of an international event

Back in 1886, the Chamber of Commerce, Industry, and Navigation of Barcelona came into being. Its main goal was to boost the economy by promoting industry and trade, which were mostly limited to the Spanish market. The plan was to attract foreigners, especially from Europe, by hosting the Universal Exhibition of 1888.

The first Universal Exhibition took up a massive space of 389,000 square meters. It spanned from the grounds of Ciutadella Park to the current location of the Hospital del Mar in Barceloneta. Literally, everything was an exhibition.

The entrance to the exhibition was marked by the *Arc de Triomf*, a creation of Barcelona architect Josep Vilaseca (1848-1910). It's one of the few structures from the event that has managed to survive the test of time. Sadly, most of the exhibition buildings have vanished over the years.

The spectacular Ciutadella fountain.

The Palau de Belles Arts, the monument to Columbus, and the Arc de Triomf, during the years of the Universal Exhibition of Barcelona.

The Palau de la Indústria, designed by Jaume Gustà, was the biggest building there, covering a whopping seventy thousand square metres. Sadly, it vanished in 1930 and now the Barcelona Zoo sits in its place.

Success in Public, Business Success

The exhibition kicked off on May 20, 1888, with the grand opening at the Palau de Belles Arts. Over the course of eight months, a staggering 400,000 people from all corners of the globe flocked to see it. The exhibition had a massive impact on Barcelona. It sparked a major industrial boom, improving the city's infrastructure and services. Thanks to this event, we got other cool things like the monument of Columbus, the avenue named after him, the Palace of Justice, the Born market, and the Moll de la Fusta. Plus, they spruced up the area between Ciutadella Park and Las Ramblas, which had been pretty run down until then.

The Eiffel Tower Could Have Been in Barcelona

Here's a fun fact: Gustave Eiffel (1832-1923), the famous French engineer, apparently pitched a wild idea for an iron tower to the exhibition organizers. They thought it was too extravagant and turned it down. But guess what? A year later, that very same structure made its debut at the Paris Universal Exhibition, and it was a hit. You probably know it as the Eiffel Tower. Originally, they planned to take it apart after the exhibition, but the public protested and it ended up becoming an iconic symbol of Paris, the city of love.

Destroy to Build: The Story of Via Laietana

The 20th century kicked off in Barcelona with some exciting urban changes. After developing the Cerdà Plan in the upper part of the city, it was time to address another strategically important decision.

❖ ❖ ❖

Via Laietana under construction.

The plan involved connecting the Eixample and the traditional parts of Barcelona to the port, a vital economic hub for the city. The bourgeoisie, who had businesses in the port, demanded it, prompting the City Council to start pulling strings to secure the necessary funds.

> **About Vocabulary**
> The street was named after the first Iberian settlers in the area.

In 1901, the council formed an economic alliance with Banco Hispano Colonial and began the construction of Via Laietana. The project required a massive budget and meant demolishing a significant number of existing structures. The anticipation surrounding the new development was so high that even King Alfonso XIII (1886-1941) visited Barcelona in March 1908. He wanted to witness the inauguration of the project, which began with the demolition of the first house at number 71 on Carrer Ample. Despite demolishing 270 buildings, the council had failed to establish an alternative plan for the displaced families around ten thousand people in total. They were left on the streets with almost nothing in the blink of an eye. This caused a sense of desolation in the city and sparked protests. However, there was no organised response, and nothing significant was achieved.

Lost Tombs and Restored Buildings

As with what happened in the Eixample, the building of the street aimed to address the area's shortcomings. This included improving the sewer system and building tunnels that would later accommodate the metro. Unfortunately, some historically valuable buildings were destroyed in the process. For instance, the convent of Sant Joan de Jerusalem, which housed Pau Claris' tomb, was demolished without rescuing the remains of the former president of the Generalitat. Thankfully, other architectural landmarks were painstakingly moved stone by stone to different parts of the city. The premises of the boilermakers and shoemakers' guilds were rebuilt in Plaça Felip Neri, and the Casa Clariana-Padellàs was relocated to Plaça del Rei, providing an opportunity to restore the grand complex.

Did you know?
The construction of buildings on Via Laietana didn't finish until 1958, just over 50 years ago.

On Via Laietana, buildings were erected to meet the business needs of the bourgeoisie living in the Eixample. Notable examples of these new centres of power and wealth included the Fomento del Trabajo Nacional, constructed between 1934 and 1936, La Caixa de Pensions, a neo-Gothic masterpiece by Enric Sagnier, and the Arrendataria de Tabacos tobacco regulators building, designed by Francesc Guàrdia i Vial.

The Tragic Week

Or How to Dodge the Draft with a Few Coins

Back in July 1909, the government rounded up reservists and shipped them off to the Melilla region, where a recent war had broken out.

❖ ❖ ❖

Spain, having lost its American colonies, turned its attention to Morocco and took control of the Rif area in 1904. The Count of Romanones (1863-1950) and two wealthy Barcelona families, the López and Güell families, set up iron and lead mines in the region. Encouraged by their discovery, they wasted no time in exploiting the mines until the Moroccans decided they deserved a piece of the action. To keep the mines under Spanish control, the conservative government of Antonio Maura (1853-1925) decided to deploy reservists.

Meanwhile, the lower classes were upset because the legislation that governed conscription allowed those who paid six thousand *reales* to dodge going to the front. Considering that the salary of a worker at the time was about twenty *reales* per day, it's clear that this was a substantial amount of money.

Several images depicting the events that unfolded during those tragic days in the city's history.

Imagine if only the richest people had the chance to dodge military conscription. Faced with this injustice, workers' groups called for a general strike on 25th July. The day ended with widespread vandalism in the city, as security forces tried to quell the protests by firing shots at the demonstrators. Witnessing the violent response from the police, the rioters put up barricades. Eventually, the government declared martial law. President Maura decided to bring in troops from other cities after the Barcelona troops refused to act against what they saw as their comrades. Once again, the clergy and religious orders in Barcelona faced difficult times. Using the argument that the Church sided with the wealthy, who could afford to exempt their sons from the war, protesters set fire to churches, convents, and monasteries. There were even disturbing scenes of men dancing with desecrated corpses from graves located in religious buildings.

After these events, the government unleashed severe and arbitrary repression. Around two thousand people, including the creator of the *Escola Moderna* (Modern School), Francesc Ferrer i Guàrdia, were arrested. He was accused, without evidence, of instigating the revolt. Ferrer i Guàrdia met his fate on October 13th of that same year, executed by firing squad on Montjuïc along with four other men. Spain and Europe were filled with outrage. In response to the international outcry over these unjustified killings, Alfonso XIII dismissed Maura.

The Tragic End of a Free Thinker

Francesc Ferrer i Guàrdia (1859-1909) was the thirteenth child of a family of winemakers from Alella, Maresme. He started working at a young age on trains bound for France and soon connected with Spanish republican exiles in Paris, sharing news about life in Catalonia with them. After getting married, he relocated to the French capital, where he where he ended up teaching Spanish. While he was there he also joined the Masons and hung out with liberals, anarchists, and socialists from different countries. As the heir to a large fortune, Ferrer i Guàrdia went back to Barcelona and fuelled by his love for teaching, established a school on Bailén Street. It was called *Escola Moderna*, a private, non-religious, co-ed, and rationalist school. He had a dedicated team that helped him spread his ideas, which he regularly published through his own publishing house. However, in 1906, his career took a hit. One of his employees, Mateo Morral, tried to assassinate Alfonso XIII on his wedding day in Madrid. Ferrer i Guàrdia was arrested and was charged with incitement and complicity but was eventually set free because of lack of evidence.

Representation of the attack against Alfonso XIII, carried out by Mateo Morral below, an employee of Francesc Ferrer i Guàrdia.

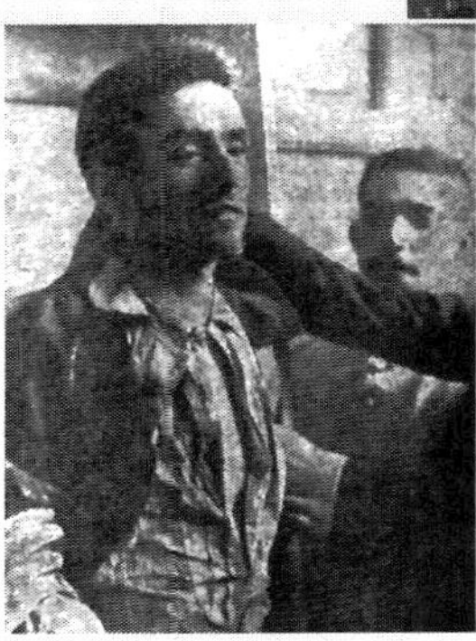

Ferrer i Guàrdia went back to Paris, where he continued to be deeply involved in pedagogy and even became the president of the International League for the Rational Education of Children. His luck took another turn when he arrived in Catalonia in June 1909, just before the Tragic Week events. This coincidence was used as proof of his guilt. Fearing further retaliation and seeing the way things were going, he went into hiding but was swiftly captured.

His defence lawyer was only given a few hours to read a massive six-hundred-page file. The trial lasted four hours and ended with a straightforward verdict: guilty. He was sentenced to death. In the final hours of his life, Ferrer i Guàrdia wrote letters to his partner and a friend. On October 13th, at Montjuïc Castle, at five in the morning, he faced the firing squad. Before he died, he declared, "I am innocent. Long live the Escola Moderna".

Plaça Catalunya (Catalonia Square), a Den of Disorder

Before the walls were completely torn down, the area where Plaça Catalunya stands today used to be a large esplanade on the outskirts of the city.

❖ ❖ ❖

Two images of Plaça Catalunya, the first in 1888 and the second in 1910.

Because of its strategic location right in front of one of the gates of the walled enclosure, all sorts of people occupied it randomly, setting up houses, circus tents, and fairground stalls.

In an attempt to bring some order to the chaos, around 1852, the Barcelona City Council came up with the idea of creating a square on this site. However, it took many years for the project to materialize. In 1888, the council held a competition, which was won by the modernist architect Pere Falqués (1850-1916). The land was taken over by the authorities, but due to various historical and political factors, its opening was repeatedly put back. Finally, on November 2nd, 1927, King Alfonso XIII inaugurated the square.

The Bad Luck of the 1929 International Exhibition

Two events led to the idea of organizing a new exhibition in Barcelona: the success of the 1888 exhibition and the desire to further expand the city. So, as early as 1905, architect Josep Puig i Cadafalch (1867-1956) proposed a project for a new international exhibition.

❖ ❖ ❖

Originally, the plan was to build the venue in the Besòs area, but in 1913, the location was changed to the Montjuïc mountain. The opening was scheduled for 1917, but due to the First World War, it had to be postponed. This setback was just the first of many, as the completion of the works in 1923 was further delayed by the establishment of Primo de Rivera's dictatorship (1870-1930).

Josep Puig i Cadafalch.

The Montjuïc Olympic Stadium was built for the 1929 Universal Exhibition.

With so many delays, the main theme of the exhibition, electricity, had lost its wow factor. To find a solution, they decided to name the event "The International Exhibition of Barcelona". But there was a snag when Seville and Bilbao also wanted to have their own exhibitions in the same year. They resolved the issue by giving each of them different titles: Seville got an "Ibero-American Exhibition", Bilbao had one focused on Machinery and Industry, and Barcelona kept the international title.

Finally, the Exhibition was inaugurated on May 20, 1929, with Alfonso XIII and Primo de Rivera in attendance. However, they had some bad luck as the New York Stock Exchange crashed on October 29, 1929, which had a drastically affected the number of visitors.

Expropriations and Architects Stopping a Train

When they first planned the exhibition space, the city council only owned 14% of the land they needed, which was around 118 hectares. So, one of the first things they did was to take over the remaining land required for the Puig i Cadafalch project.

A large team of architects, including Puig i Cadafalch, Lluís Domènech i Montaner, Enric Sagnier, and August Font, together with their teams, collaborated on the project and designed all the buildings.

Some of the structures that were built for the exhibition included the Palau Nacional, the *Estadi Olímpic* (Olympic Stadium), the *Font Màgica*, the *Teatre Grec,* and Poble Espanyol.

The exhibition, which had cost a whopping 130 million pesetas, ended up in the red. It didn't have the same economic success as the previous one, but it did gain some social and international recognition for Barcelona. Unlike the first exhibition, the buildings in this second one remained intact in the city's landscape.

Did you know?
The Montjuïc funicular and the Port Cable Car, which can be accessed from the port, also date back to this time although the latter couldn't be officially opened until 1931.

On the left, you can see a panoramic view of the 1929 Universal Exhibition. It featured various constructions, including the Montjuïc fountains and the National Palace located above, which were both inaugurated during this event.

SOME INFO

The musical *Flor de nit* (*Flower of the Night*) by the theatre company Dagoll Dagom is all about the vibes in Barcelona during the International Exhibition.

From Dictatorship to Republic

Alfonso XIII and Miguel Primo de Rivera.

Miguel Primo de Rivera, the Captain General of Catalonia, came to power in Spain with the backing of the monarchy, the far-right, and some members of the Catalan bourgeoisie. Catalonia faced quick and surgical actions: repression of the labor movement, banning of political parties, dissolution of the *Mancomunidad* (association of local authorities), and the banning of the Catalan language and symbols like the anthem and flag. After seven years, Primo de Rivera lost all support and resigned in January 1930. The king appointed General Dámaso Berenguer (1873-1953) as the new head of government, attempting to steer the situation with a softer dictatorship known as the *Dictablanda*, but without success. Exploiting the government's weakness, Republican parties gathered in Donostia to discuss establishing the Republic. Berenguer's government collapsed a year after its proclamation, and Admiral Juan Bautista Aznar-Cabañas (1860-1933) took over as the new head of government. However, destiny had already been sealed. After municipal elections where Republicans emerged victorious in almost every city, Alfonso XIII was forced to go into exile.

The Most Feared Storm in Catalonia

The Spanish Republic shifts from left-wing governments Alcalá Zamora, Azaña to confused governments Lerroux, with a significant rise of the right-wing.

❖ ❖ ❖

In Barcelona, Macià boldly declared the Republic on his own, but he quickly had to backtrack. It was then that his party, Esquerra Republicana de Catalunya, realised the need to create an Autonomy Statute. After the text was approved in 1932, Macià became the president of the Generalitat, and Catalonia once again had its own government and parliament to make laws on matters outlined in the statute. When Macià passed away in 1933, Lluís Companys took over Catalan executive power.

Celebrations following the proclamation of the Second Spanish Republic, in Barcelona in 1931.

But the sense of freedom didn't last long. The rise of the right-wing in the Spanish government created tensions that led to the imprisonment of Companys and his advisors. In February 1936, everything changed once again when the Popular Front emerged victorious in the state-level legislative elections and the Leftist Front in Catalonia. Companys and his advisors were set free, but the return to normality was short-lived. In fact, on July 17th, a military uprising took place in the Spanish territories of Morocco, marking the beginning of the Civil War.

The Long Absence of Macià

Francesc Macià passed away on December 25th, 1933. His body was laid to rest in the mausoleum at Plaça de la Fe in the Montjuïc cemetery, while his heart was entrusted to Josep Tarradellas for safekeeping.

As Franco's troops were about to enter Barcelona, Tarradellas and other politicians secretly relocated Macià's body to another mausoleum to prevent any desecration. They chose the mausoleum of the Collaso Gil brothers, who had no close relatives, ensuring a secure location. The body remained there from 1939, while Tarradellas went into exile with the president's heart.

Francesc Macià talking to the people.

During the Transition period, Tarradellas handed Macià's heart to his daughter Maria on October 9th, 1979. The next day, the body was returned to its original mausoleum.

A Barracks Packed with Military Gear

Back in 1929, they built the Bailén barracks in the Sant Andreu neighbourhood, smack between Gran de Sant Andreu Street and Palomar Street. These barracks were meant to house a whole bunch of soldiers and their weapons, and they started operating in 1934.

❖ ❖ ❖

When the military uprising kicked off on July 18, 1936, General Justo Legorburu, who was in charge of the barracks, locked himself in there, ready to unleash hell on Barcelona. But the anarchist militants and the pro-Republic folks in the neighbourhood knew they had to act fast and take control of the place.

Anarchist groups actively participated in the attack on the barracks.

So, the Republic's planes bombed the barracks, making it easier for the CNT and FAI forces to storm in. After a gruelling two-day siege, in the wee hours of July 20, the barracks' officers surrendered. The militants managed to get their hands on the military gear before the Civil Guard, sent by the Generalitat, took over. That move seriously boosted the militia's arsenal.

The Beginning of the End

On that fateful day, July 18, 1936, Franco took charge of the rebel troops in Morocco, while General Emilio Mola did the same up north on the peninsula. Meanwhile, in Barcelona, the military rose up the next day, but they faced a strong resistance from the public order

General Emilio Mola.

Franco took charge of the rebel troops in Morocco. In Barcelona, the CNT occupied the house of moderate Catalan politician Francesc Cambó.

forces controlled by the Generalitat, the working masses, and the Civil Guard, who remained loyal to the legitimate government of the Spanish Republic. The rebels had to surrender, but there was no going back.

A Fancy House for the CNT-FAI

On the same day, July 19th, a group of armed union members from the CNT stormed the home of politician Francesc Cambó. His house was located in the same building as the employers' organization Fomento del Trabajo Nacional National Work Promotion on Via Laietana. It is said that the militiamen, who came from the outskirts of the city, were amazed by the mansion's luxurious facilities. It is believed that Federica Montseny herself, who would later become the Minister of Health, visited the house and provided some guidelines for its organization. The following day, the union members declared the building confiscated and established the CNT-FAI House until the end of the conflict. After the war, the building was returned to Fomento del Trabajo to be used as before.

A joke about the conservatism of Francesc Cambó, published in the Spanish liberal newspaper *El Imparcial*.

The Most Savage Bombings

From March 16th to 18th, 1938, there were non-stop bombings for over forty hours. There were twelve attacks only three hours apart from each other. The outcome was a massacre: over seven hundred people killed, around a thousand injured, and two hundred buildings completely destroyed.

❖ ❖ ❖

This kind of operation was known as "saturation bombing" with the aim of demoralising the population, disrupting the normal lives of citizens, and preventing emergency services like firefighters and ambulances from effectively responding under the rain of bombs.

Italian, German, and Spanish planes mercilessly bombed the civilian population of Barcelona.

Out of those three days, the most devastating was the 17th, when five Savoia-79 planes dropped a total of eight bombs weighing two hundred and fifty kilograms each, a hundred bombs weighing one hundred kilograms each, and twelve incendiary explosives weighing twenty kilograms each over the heart of Barcelona. One of the bombs hit a truck filled with trinitrotoluene at the intersection of Balmes and Gran Via streets. The resulting explosion was so massive that even the pilots were astonished by the impact. The area was completely obliterated, engulfed in an endless column of smoke from the fire, and leaving a deep crater.

Did you know?
From the start of the war until January 24th, 1939, Barcelona got hit with a whopping 385 bombings, mostly carried out by the Italian air force, with a little help from the Germans and Francoist forces. A total of 1.903 bombs rained down on the city's roofs. And get this, a staggering 70% of all the bombings during the war targeted Barcelona.

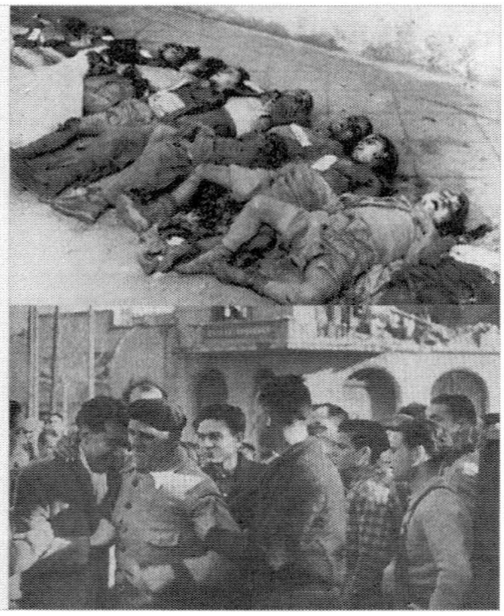

The casualties were numerous. Not only did the bombs wreak havoc on the city's residents and people out for a walk, but one of them even landed on a bus packed with passengers, turning it into a horrific pile of charred and twisted metal.

Twenty Kilometres of Tunnels to Shelter from the Bombs

The Francoist faction instigated the tragic practice of bombing the civilian population. Although it may be hard to believe, it wasn't until the Spanish Civil War that this type of bombing began, devised by the German Nazis.

The new war strategy, 'saturation bombing', prompted the mobilisation of the entire city. It was necessary to create a network of shelters, and this was done by taking advantage of the existing social fabric in Catalan society, such as various committees or neighbourhood associations.

With the first bombings, the people of Barcelona understood that they had to find shelter underground. Initially, metro stations and the Sarrià train station became improvised air-raid shelters. Acting swiftly, in September 1936, the Barcelona City Council created a passive defence unit against aerial attacks and organized a network of night watchmen, chemists, and hospitals

Tunnels of the Anti-Air Raid Shelter 307, on Nou de La Rambla Street.

Below, the children of a destroyed school in Barcelona cry on the street.

that stayed on alert in case of emergencies. They also encouraged residents to build shelters in each neighbourhood. It was the job of the community to come together and find collective solutions. Men took up positions on the front lines or took care of defence, while everyone worked together to plan and construct shelters. People used whatever materials they could find, such as bricks from barricades, stones from destroyed houses, and remains from previous bombings.

The population was informed about the steps to take in case of a bombing, and sirens were installed to signal when it was time to seek shelter and when the danger had passed. In June 1937, the Generalitat extended the Barcelona experience to the rest of Catalonia. The government provided subsidies for neighbourhood initiatives, prepared existing spaces for use, and ensured the electricity supply. The remaining tasks were taken care of by the population.

SOME INFO

In Barcelona, an underground network of shelters was created, and some of them were interconnected. By the end of the war, there were approximately twenty kilometres of tunnels that could accommodate between two hundred thousand and three hundred thousand refugees.

And Barcelona also Falls

So, after a series of painful losses, both the Spanish Republican government and the Basque government decided to move their capitals to Barcelona. The Battle of the Ebro, which lasted for a gruelling four months, ended in defeat for the Republicans and dealt a fatal blow to their cause. From that point on, the Republican army could only hold on and resist, lacking the strength to launch any significant attacks.

Exhausted and beaten militiamen fleeing towards the border with France, seeking refuge.

Exile of the militiamen and their families.

And then, on January 26, 1939, Franco's troops triumphantly entered Barcelona. They marched down the Gran Via with their heads held high, while the weary militiamen trudged along, defeated and downtrodden, heading for the border. Some people took to the streets to enthusiastically welcome the occupiers. Behind the shattered city walls, there were others who had been defeated. From Barcelona, the Nationalist army advanced towards the French border, and on 1 April 1939, the conflict finally came to an end. Franco had arrived, and he was here to stay for a very long time.

The graffiti that can currently be seen in Sant Josep Oriol square.

Did you know?
The Municipal Institute of Urban Landscape and Quality of Life of Barcelona has restored the graffiti.

The Square of the Unknown Militiaman

Those were some rough days, I tell you. Barcelona was a total mess, with ruins scattered everywhere. But amidst all that, you can still find some heartfelt memories. Check out Sant Josep Oriol square, right by the Pi church in Ciutat Vella. Back in 1937, someone grabbed a brush and some tar and wrote on the church wall: "Plaça del Milicia Desconegut" (Square of the Unknown Militiaman). It was their way of honouring the brave militiamen who fought for the Republic. They had stood up for democracy, armed and ready. Unfortunately, many of them lost their lives or were unjustly exiled. And not to forget the thousands who were captured and mistreated in Franco's prisons. This simple tribute stands there, with no fanfare or ceremony, just to keep their memory alive. In 1939, the sign was painted over, but bit by bit, it's re-emerged like it's trying to remind us of those forgotten heroes.

2. Curiosities of Barcelona's streets and buildings

Streets, Squares, Buildings, and Parks to Live in

If we tally up all the different names found throughout the city, including squares, passages, and streets, we'd discover around five thousand of them. Some names are short and sweet, like the eight single-letter ones or the twenty-four numbered ones. Others have a religious theme, with 179 streets dedicated to saints. If we were to list them alphabetically, the first and last addresses would provide an interesting contrast. We'd start with Abadessa Olzet Street, a charming little street in Pedralbes with grand houses, lavish pools, and beautiful gardens. And at the end of the list, we'd have Zurbarán Square, a dark and grey place flanked by two massive apartment blocks. This square is often used by neighbours and visitors to park their vehicles while visiting the Vall d'Hebron Hospital's emergency room. A place where, surely, no tourist would stick their head in.

❖ ❖ ❖

The Most Famous Gallows in Catalonia

In Spanish, when we want to say that someone or something is very far away, we use the phrase: "Está en el quinto pino" (They're in the fifth pine tree). In Catalan, the same expression is translated as "la quinta forca," which means the fifth gallows". We might not know which specific pine tree the Spanish phrase refers to, but we do know the origin of the fifth gallows in Catalonia.

When we think about Barcelona, various iconic landmarks might come to mind: the statue of Columbus at the end of La Rambla, the impressive facade of La Pedrera on Passeig de Gràcia, or the towering spires of the Sagrada Familia. However, the city's landscapes haven't always been the same, and the common sights have changed over time to suit different needs. In the past, the city had a lot more to do with executions and the gallows than with picturesque views.

During the reign of the Roman Emperor Constantine 272-337, when Christianity was tolerated for practical reasons, he imposed restrictions on death by crucifixion. But the Romans, not satisfied with that punishment alone, came up with another gruesome contraption: the gallows. It was one thing to be religiously devoted and another to be legally flexible in Roman society.

Barcelona, being a good student of Latin, had gallows scattered throughout its streets. Just like passing by a pastry shop nowadays, many people used to encounter these eerie wooden structures on a daily basis.

The city even had five permanent gallows. They were strategically placed on busy roads that travellers had to cross to enter the urban area. The authorities of that time probably wanted to ensure that anyone entering the city was well aware of the consequences if they dared to break the law. So, where were these gallows located? Well, they could be found at Pla de Palau, the Sant Antoni gate, Pla de la Boqueria, the jurisdictional boundary with the town of Sants, and at the Turó de Finestrelles. The last one, being quite remote from the others, was also known as Cerro de la Trinidad. Considering the locations of the first four gallows, it's surprising just how far away the fifth one was. No wonder people referred to it as "the farthest away" whenever they needed to express a great distance.

El Pla de Palau at the beginning of the 20th century.

Neither Nuclear nor Waste nor Gallows

Demands may change over time, but the core issue remains the same. While people today may protest against the location of prisons, nuclear power plants, or waste incinerators, in the 14th century, the complaints of some residents were aimed at the gallows.

El Pla de Palau today.

Did you know?
Back in feudal times, lords had the power to erect gallows on their lands to show off their authority.

This was the case for the people living around Pla de Palau, where now the Spanish government delegation is located. This place used to be swarming with ships constantly loading and unloading goods, including lots of fish. But the smell of decaying bodies since it was common to leave the executed bodies hanging for a few days to scare the locals probably didn't attract many buyers. Around 1382, the residents of Pla de Palau got fed up with all the spoiled meat and asked King Peter the Ceremonious to move the gallows to another part of the city. Whether in the centre or on the outskirts, the gallows disappeared from Barcelona on April 28th, 1832, thanks to a decree that banned this type of execution.

SOME INFO

Gallows came in various forms: permanent, temporary, and even portable you never knew when you might need them .

If You Want a Wall, Build It

In 801, the Franks officially kicked out the Muslims from Barcelona. However, even after almost a century of living in the city, many Muslims chose to stay despite losing their institutions and positions. The deep roots they had established with Barcelona over such a long time were stronger than the power struggles over territory.

But the Franks didn't fully trust the Muslims who wanted to stay, so they decided to let them remain, but not inside the walls. That's how two new suburbs popped up in Barcelona. The first settlement was by the beach, although we're not exactly sure where it was, but it probably covered a big area around the streets of Ample and Passeig de Colom. They named this place "The Saracen Neighbourhood".

The second settlement, on the other side of the Rambla, was called Raval (Arrabal). It had lots of gardens and houses where peasants, artisans, and blacksmiths lived outside the walls. The neighbourhood grew so much that in the 14th century, there were almost as many people outside the walls as inside. Then, Peter the Ceremonious decided to build a new fortified enclosure. Some say he allowed Raval to join the protected city because of all the gardens it had - if there was a siege, they could rely on the food supply for a while. Others think the people of Raval pressured the king to let them in. How could they have so much influence over the king, you ask? Well, let's not forget that it was the citizens themselves who built the walls: if you include us, we'll support you; if you exclude us, you're on your own. Whatever the case, with the expansion of the walls, Raval became part of Barcelona.

About Vocabulary
"Arrabal" comes from the Hispanic-Arabic word *rabad* and refers to the part of the population living outside the city walls.

You can see the remains of walls on the side of the Church of Sant Agustí in Raval.

Becoming a Woman with a Change of Shoes

Your probably familiar with the fact that our towns and cities have streets named after old trades practiced there. You've got Clockmakers' Street, Coachmakers' Street, Doctors' Street, and so on. But there's one street whose meaning might not be as well-known: Tapineria Street.

In the Middle Ages, a woman couldn't wear *chapines* until she was married.

Now, here's the interesting part. Tapineria Street is linked to these cork sandals called *chapines* or *tapins* in Catalan . These sandals were lined with leather and cloth, and they had three or four cork soles to keep the feet dry and make women's figures appear slimmer. Back in the Middle Ages, unmarried women couldn't wear *chapines*.

About Vocabulary
Apparently, the name *chapin* refers to the noise that this type of footwear made when you walked.

Public Beatings to Punish Crimes

Now, let's talk about Bòria Street. It was the first street to expand beyond the city walls, right in front of the north gate. It was the busiest street because it led to Gaul. So, many important people who wanted to conquer, help, or simply visit the city had to pass through there.

Here's an interesting fact: The prison was located in Plaza del Rei, close to Bòria Street. It led to a strange tradition known as *Passar Bòria avall* (Pass down Bòria). Basically, they publicly punished criminals by beating them and forcing them to walk along certain streets, including Bòria on foot or on horseback. If someone was sentenced to death, their journey would end at Pla de

Representation of the *Passar Bòria avall*, and, on the right, the street of La Bòria today.

Palau, where the gloomy gallows awaited them. As for small-time criminals, it was hoped that the experience would scare them enough to think twice before committing another crime. This practice continued until the early 19th century.

About Vocabulary
They say bòria means a fancy way of saying a neighbourhood or suburb.

SOME INFO

Back when hanging was still a thing, many believed that the rope used for the execution brought good luck. So, it was common to see people picking up bits of the ropes used at places like Pla de Palau or the current Plaça de Espanya, where some executions took place.

The House of *Pia Almoina:* Feeding One Hundred Poor People a Day

The street called Baixada de la Canonja, next to the cathedral, got its name from the Order of Canons who lived there. In 1009, the religious community running the Pia Almoina building got a wonderful gift. A generous merchant named Robert donated to provide meals for a hundred poor people every day. Right in front of that building, you had all sorts of people lining up. We're talking about people who didn't have much money, sick people, and travellers who needed some grub after their long journeys.

Did you know? Back in 1369, the building where these 'men of God' had lived got torn down. They put up the Diocesan Museum in its place, which is still there today.

The Jewish Quarter: aka the Rulers' Private Bank

Out of all the Jewish quarters in Catalan territories like Girona, Lleida, Montblanc, and Tortosa, the one in Barcelona was the biggest and most populated. Back in the 13th century, there were around five thousand people living there, which was a big deal at the time.

That area was basically a hotspot for merchants. The Jews had the dough, and the rulers were always turning to them for cash to fund their military campaigns. But even though the Jews played a big role in Barcelona's economy, they weren't fully integrated with the rest of the city. They weren't even allowed to use the same water sources as the Christians. And on the flip side, Christians couldn't enter their quarter because the Jewish residents liked their privacy. Unfortunately, when the Jews were massacred in 1391, the whole neighbourhood went down with them. Despite some efforts by the monarchs, the *Call* (Jewish Quarter) of Barcelona never bounced back to its former glory.

SOME INFO

The Jewish people in Barcelona used to speak Catalan and Hebrew, which was quite unusual because most Jewish communities would adopt the language spoken in the place they lived, while Hebrew was mainly reserved for religious purposes.

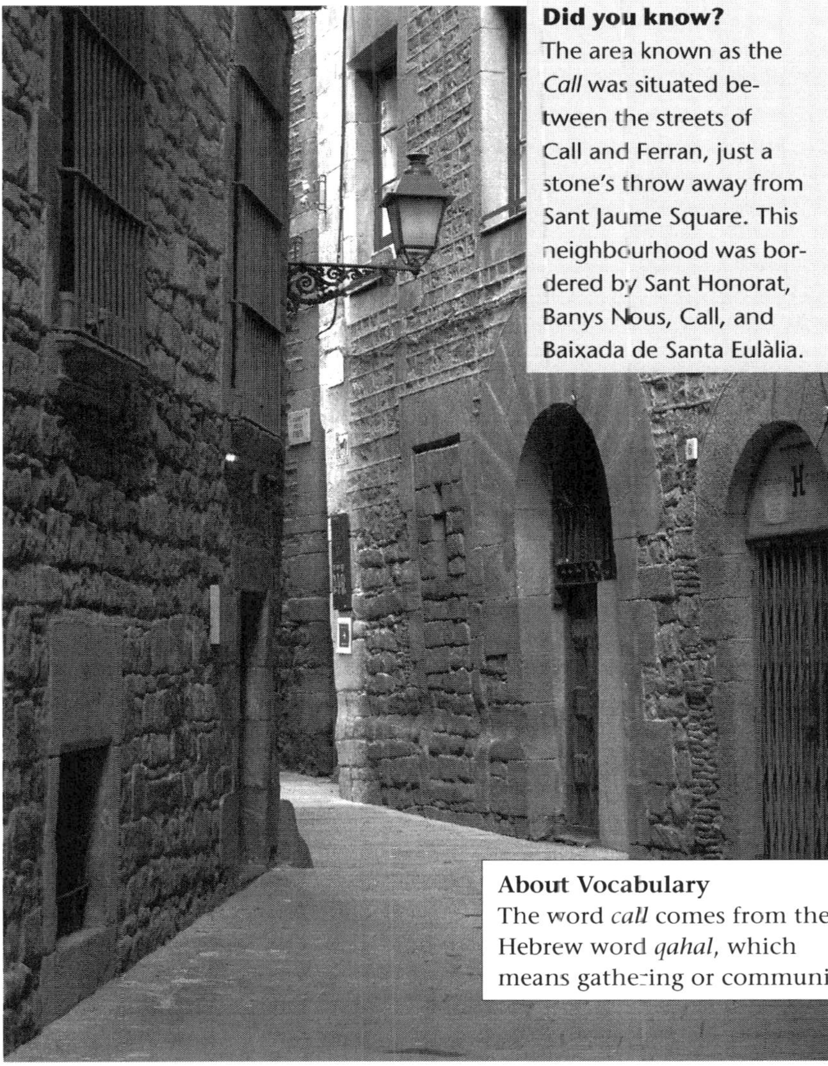

Did you know?
The area known as the *Call* was situated between the streets of Call and Ferran, just a stone's throw away from Sant Jaume Square. This neighbourhood was bordered by Sant Honorat, Banys Nous, Call, and Baixada de Santa Eulàlia.

About Vocabulary
The word *call* comes from the Hebrew word *qahal*, which means gathering or community.

Marlet Street where it meets Sant Domènec del Call.

Avinyó Was a Gentleman

Speaking of the *Call*, let me tell you this cool legend about the quarter. Joan Amades tells the story about a real devout and kind-hearted bloke from Barcelona. He wasn't afraid to talk to Jewish people, even when others wouldn't give them the time of day. He even went as far as to talk to a Jewish man whom other Jews shunned. Everyone thought he was a bit nuts, but he didn't care.

Avinyó Street and Verònica Square.

Now, one day, this Jew that everyone shunned got sick. He knew he was about to kick the bucket, so he asked his only friend, for a favour. He wanted him to hire a town crier to announce his death to everyone and let them know that whoever attended his funeral could have his stuff.

Being the good-hearted guy that he was, he paid for the town crier himself. But the news didn't really spread very far, because he was the only one who showed up at the funeral.

Feeling sad about the loss, Avinyó that was the man's last name went to the dead man's house to collect a few old things that were supposed to be scattered around. But guess what? He found a secret basement under the mattress, jam-packed with riches! Avinyó became one of the richest landowners in Barcelona after that. He bought up so many properties on his street that they eventually named it after him. Talk about karma.

Making Noise Outside the Walls

If you have a noisy neighbour, you'll understand. The guild of boilermakers had initially set themselves up on central Ferran Street. But their noisy practices, *bang, bang, bang,* tortured the neighbours so much that they had to move away from the city centre. Carrying their pots and pans, the hammer men left the Trinitarian Fathers' convent now the church of Sant Jaume and ended up on Bòria Street, outside the walls.

Later, the coppersmiths also moved to Bòria, along with the bell ringers and other metalworkers. We don't know how the existing residents of that street reacted, but one thing is certain: it would be impossible to concentrate during the day.

Did you know?
We know that the guild of boilermakers has existed, at least, since the year 1275 because there was one in the Consell de Cent held that year.

The Cathedral of Small Stories

Barcelona Cathedral before its current façade was built.

Third Time's a Charm

The Cathedral of the Holy Cross and Saint Eulalia is situated in a large open space, the Cathedral Square. The original paleo-Christian structure was later expanded with a Romanesque addition. However, in 1298, it was decided to further enlarge the building, resulting in the construction of the current Gothic cathedral. This third and final reconstruction of the monumental building took place over the course of the 13th, 14th, and 15th centuries. But the current façade was only made possible thanks to the generosity of businessman Manuel Girona, who financed all the expenses during the Universal Exhibition of 1888.

Construction of the dome of Barcelona Cathedral, between 1906 and 1913.

According to legend, the cathedral was erected in this location because there used to be an old pine forest where Santiago supposedly preached the good news of Christ for the first time in Barcelona.

SOME INFO

According to some accounts, the initial two buildings, which were smaller in size compared to the current cathedral, had their main entrance where the apse is currently situated.

A Martyr from The Plains of Barcelona

Christianity spread like wildfire between the 1st and 3rd centuries, starting from Rome and reaching Africa, and then making its way to Hispania. Barcelona, with its proximity to the Mediterranean and the Via Augusta, became a hotspot for the Christian teachings brought by traders and travellers. The followers of this growing religion, including our own ancestors, played a crucial role in paving the way for change. One of the most well-known among them is Saint Eulalia, the martyr who now lends her name to the city's cathedral. Let me share with you the tale of this remarkable woman.

Diocletian, the Christians' archenemy.

A Show Unfit for Kids

In the year 303, the Roman emperor Diocletian unleashed severe persecution against Christians. His henchman, the prefect Dacian, took his orders seriously and organized a series of public rituals in Barcelona to honour the Roman gods. The intention was clear: to put a halt to the spread of Christianity. Whether people liked it or not, they were forced to attend these gruesome spectacles, even the children. Eulalia, a girl not even thirteen years old, found herself in that dreadful place as circumstances dictated. However, she couldn't contain herself. With a loud voice, she shouted her unwavering faith in Christ and asserted the rights of citizens to embrace her doctrine.

Dacian was taken aback by such audacity and had her punished with a flogging. But Eulalia remained resolute and refused to retract her words. The prefect then subjected her to thirteen tortures, including more whippings, burns, amputations, and even flea bites.

The Legend Comes to Life

According to popular belief, when they set the young girl on fire, the flames that engulfed her body turned against the soldiers who stood around her. In the midst of the crowd's fright, Eulalia's soul left her mouth in the form of a white dove and rose up to the sky. Once crucified, the happiness of eternity made her smile while a pure white snow covered the city of Barcelona. At midnight, some Christians stole her body and buried it in an unknown location so that the Romans wouldn't attempt to desecrate it. In the year 878, the remains of the girl were found in Santa Maria de las Arenas, where the church of Santa Maria del Mar currently stands, and they were transferred to the cathedral. It was then that Saint Eulalia became the patron saint of Barcelona.

Did you know?
Santa Eulàlia used to be the sole patron saint of the city until the Modern Age. After that, she had to share the title with the Virgin of La Mercè.

You can find this depiction of Sant Eulàlia at the Church of the Josepets in Gràcia.

A Saint Full of Questions

During the Early Middle Ages, it was common for hagiographic figures to be duplicated, and it seems that the story of the brave girl from Barcelona might not have actually existed. Her legend could have been born from a mix-up with the story of Saint Eulalia of Mérida, who experienced similar martyrdoms and shared the same name as the Catalan saint.

The Cathedral's geese symbolize purity.

The Cathedral with Geese

At her home, Eulàlia took care of her family's geese. To honour her and her age at the time of her death, there are thirteen geese around the lake in the cathedral's courtyard. These birds are white, symbolizing her purity.

SOME INFO

Saint Eulalia is often shown with an X-shaped cross and a palm branch, which represents her martyrdom.

The King's Private Door

Let's go back to the cathedral, where there are still some hidden secrets. You can discover some of them on one of the walls of Sant Iu Square. There's a door hanging in mid-air there. This door used to connect the Palau Reial Mayor to one of its rooms via a bridge and provided a direct entrance for the kings to the church, so they didn't have to mingle with the common people.

The door of Sant Iu Square.

The Snail of Discord

On the right tower behind the cathedral, you'll find a carved snail. According to popular belief, it represents a psychological battle fought by a betrayed husband. The husband suspected his wife of having an affair, and to let her know that he was aware of it, he decided to carve a snail on the wall. The snail might seem small and vulnerable, but it can hide its horns whenever it wants. Another theory, less dramatic, suggests that the snails if you look closely, there's more than one were carved as a reminder of a plague caused by these molluscs while the temple was being built.

What could be the meaning of the Cathedral's snail?

Gargoyles: Protectors or Demons?

No one really knows for sure what gargoyles were all about. Some people think these scary stone creatures were meant to guard the temples they perched on. With their fierce faces and gaping, torn mouths, they were meant to scare away any sinners who dared approach the holy buildings. But there are others who argue that gargoyles were meant to represent demons trying to break free from the church.

One of the Cathedral's gargoyles.

According to the legend of Barcelona Cathedral, the gargoyles adorning it are actually witches and evil spirits who got turned to stone for mocking the Holy Form during the Corpus procession. As punishment, they were condemned to drink rainwater whether they were thirsty or not.

SOME INFO

By the way, Barcelona Cathedral has a whopping 250 gargoyles, but not all of them look terrifying or menacing. In fact, there are three that depict friendly and noble creatures from our imagination: a bull, an elephant, and the most mystical of all, a unicorn. The meaning of these animals varies depending on who's looking at them.

About Vocabulary
Those figures that aren't used for water drainage aren't technically gargoyles, but they're called chimeras.

Did you know?
Gargoyles didn't exist before the 12th century. Those early Romanesque buildings were so basic that they didn't bother with roof drains. Oh, and every gargoyle is unique—no repeats!

The Stolen Finger of Saint Eulalia

Right in front of the main entrance of the first walled enclosure, next to Bòria Street, there was this square where the local peasants sold their wares, just like in the other city entrances. Because of all the trading going on there, people started calling it the Wheat or Kids' Square, but that name didn't last long after something miraculous happened.

Back in 878, they found the remains of Saint Eulalia in the old church of Santa Maria de las Arenas. They decided to move her body to the cathedral. So, the story goes that when the procession carrying the girl's remains arrived at Plaça del Blat (Wheat Square), the coffin suddenly became really heavy, and nobody could budge it.

Plaça de l'Àngel in 1895.

People were all confused and wondering what on Earth was going on. They started praying and, wouldn't you know it, their prayers were answered. An angel showed up and basically pointed at one of the canons who was walking with the coffin. The poor man confessed that he had swiped one of the saint's fingers to keep as a relic. Eulàlia, being the kind saint she was, wanted to enter the cathedral intact, so she let them continue the procession once the finger was returned. And from then on, Plaça del Blat became known as Plaça de l'Àngel (Angel Square).

When Owning Weapons at Home Was a Must

Back in the 13th century, scattered around the Plain of Barcelona, there were some villages and hamlets surviving on farming and taking care of livestock. Since they didn't need all the crops for themselves, many people decided to head to Barcelona and

An engraving from 1535 which clearly shows the boundaries of medieval Barcelona. The artwork is by the artists Jan Cornelius Vermeyen and Frans Hogenber, and is preserved at the Hebrew University in Jerusalem.

sell their harvest surplus, even if it meant having to give up a few coins. Back in the day, people in Gràcia, Sants, Sarrià, Sant Gervasi de Cassoles, and Sant Martí de Provençals had to pay a tribute to the Barcelona City Council if they wanted to trade the stuff they made in the city and its surrounding areas.

Even though these towns were outside the city walls, the counts protected them. But the residents still had to keep weapons like swords, spears, or crossbows at home to defend their territory. It's hard to imagine the government nowadays making everyone keep weapons in their homes, right?

Did you know?
Over time, the zone around Barcelona expanded so much that a century later, Horta, Sant Just Desvern, Sant Joan Despí, Sant Boi de Llobregat, Badalona, and Sant Feliu de Llobregat joined the group of towns that had to pay tribute to the city.

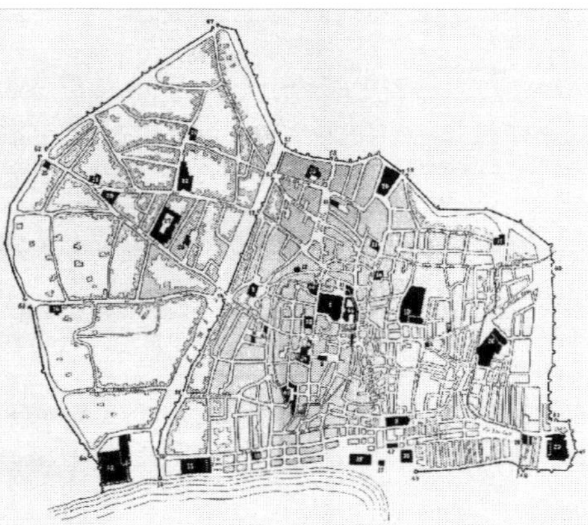

Miraculous Beans in The Plains of Barcelona

Santa Eulàlia isn't the only example of hagiographic personality duplication that went down in Christian history. Right alongside her, straddling that fine line between myth and reality, we've got San Medir. He was a humble peasant who, just like the girl from Barcelona's plains, was also the protagonist of a miracle.

According to the story, Medir lived in a farmhouse halfway between Barcelona and Sant Cugat. He had a little plot of land right by the Roman road. Now, we all know how the prefect Dacian treated Christians back in the day. And since the Romans hated crosses, the Bishop of Barcelona, Severus, decided to take that road to escape certain death.

Mosaic depicting the legend of Saint Medir and Bishop Severus.

Did you know?
In Catalonia, Saint Medir is the patron saint of farmers.

The religious procession, on its way out of the city, crossed paths with Medir. He was out there in his garden, planting beans. The bishop straight up told him that if Dacian's henchmen came asking which way they went, he had to tell the truth, no hesitation. Medir was ready to die for his Christian faith. But here's the twist—when the bishop left, those beans of his miraculously started growing like crazy. It was as if the peasant had planted them long before.

Sure enough, a little while later, the soldiers showed up and started interrogating Medir. Following the bishop's orders, the man told them that while he was busy planting his beans, the bishop and the other believers had passed by. But when the soldiers saw those flourishing crops, they thought Medir was making fun of them and promptly chopped off his head.

But he wasn't the only victim. On the way to Sant Cugat, the soldiers came across Sever and hammered a big nail into his head, killing him stone dead. Since then, San Sever has been the patron saint of headaches. Years later, they built a hermitage in his honour in the miraculous field of San Medir.

SOME INFO

In ancient times, the peasants believed that when a field became barren, they had to sow St. Medir's beans to make the land fertile again.

The Sick Man Who Started a Tradition

In 1830, there was a baker named Josep Vidal i Gramés. He had a business near Fontana and one day he found out that he was seriously ill. He was desperate and made a promise to St. Medir. He said that if he recovered from his illness by the following 3rd March, which was the saint's feast day, he would go to the hermitage to thank him and share the good news with everyone. Miraculously, he was cured, and true to his word, he went to the hermitage to express his gratitude. To catch people's attention, he even gave out sweets he'd made himself to everyone he met.

The next year, the baker made the journey again, but this time he wasn't alone. His family and friends joined him, riding on horses. As the years went by, more and more people from Gràcia joined the unique walk, each with their own promises. And as the group grew, the sound of music filled the air.

Did you know?
The worship of St. Medir was forgotten for a long time. It wasn't until the 19th century that the people of Gràcia and Sant Gervasi started celebrating the pilgrimage, which eventually became very popular among the residents.

Children asking for sweets on San Medir's Day in the Gràcia neighbourhood.

Tallers Street heading in the direction of La Rambla.

About Vocabulary
According to Víctor Balaguer, the name *Tallers* is connected to the verb *tallar* to cut because apparently, people who sliced meat used to live there.

The Thousand and One Moves of the Cheerful Women

By the 14th century, Tallers Street was one of the areas with the worst reputation in the city. It got so scandalous that in 1350, Peter the Ceremonious banned brothels from being located within forty steps of the churches near La Rambla.

We don't know where the expelled girls went, but we do know that the tradition remained. There's evidence of a brothel in the same area in the late 16th century, but once again, the ladies had to pack their bags and go. The General Study had been built nearby, and the authorities didn't want the morals of the well-to-do students to be compromised. But traditions are hard to get rid of, and by 1860, the place was still known as the brothel courtyard. In fact, we could say that the tradition has persisted till today.

Did you know?
The University of Barcelona has a long history that goes way back to Martí the Humane's reign. He wanted to establish a medical school in the city, and so he did. Then, in 1450, Alfonso the Magnanimous founded the General Study of Barcelona, which was essentially the early version of the university we have today. The building, situated in the part of La Rambla known as "de los Estudios" precisely because of the university, became less important when Felipe V imposed restrictions. Eventually, in 1843, the building was torn down.

Back when Barcelona had gates

In the past, Barcelona was a walled city with gates that closed around half past six in the afternoon. The only exception was the Portal de l'Àngel, which stayed open until seven. About fifteen minutes before closing time, a drummer would play his instrument to remind everyone to enter the city. However, at three in the morning, the Portal de l'Àngel would reopen temporarily to allow carts to remove trash and transport the bodies of those who couldn't afford a proper burial. People had to wait until half past six in the morning to enter the city gates again.

Portal de l'Àngel seen from Plaça Catalunya.

Barcelona and Its Guardian Angel

Sant Vicenç.

Back in the day, this place used to be known as the Orbs the blind because it attracted a large crowd of blind people, disabled individuals, and beggars. One day, Vicent Ferrer, a Dominican from Valencia (1350-1419), was returning from preaching and as he entered the city through the portal, he saw an angel holding a sword. Curious, Ferrer asked him, "What are you doing here?". The angel replied, "I protect Barcelona on orders from the Highest". The future saint was astonished by the vision, but not many people believed him when he shared the story. However, during a plague outbreak in the city, someone remembered the angel, and desperate people started offering him gifts. Miraculously, the plague started to recede. The city leaders then built a chapel with a large statue of the guardian angel, and the portal became known as *del Àngel*.

The First Tax Evasions

The Pla de la Boqueria was situated right in front of one of the gates of the ancient city. It served as an entrance and exit point of the walled area, and there were terrifying gallows there. Being strategically located, it became a popular spot for street vendors, farmers from nearby towns, and rural homesteads. They preferred to sell their fruits, vegetables, and grains outside the walls to avoid paying taxes on their goods. Over time,

The Pla de la Boqueria in the late 19th century.

Where the Boqueria market stands today, there used to be the Sant Josep convent, which disappeared back in 1835.

all sorts of artisans, fabric merchants, and even healers with magical remedies for various ailments joined them. The market grew so much that even tooth-pullers, jesters, storytellers, and, of course, thieves could be found.

A Market Was Born from a Convent

While the vendors kept on trading outside to dodge paying, life within the walls moved forward. In the La Rambla area, in 1586, they built a new religious building: the Sant Josep Convent. However, it met its demise in 1835 during the chaos that engulfed the streets of Barcelona for a few days. Instead, an open space surrounded by a colonnade took its place. And that plain became the new spot for those who had been avoiding taxes until then. They had to move their stalls inside and presumably pay what was owed. The space was designed by Francesc Daniel Molina (1812-1867), an architect who took inspiration from the work of John Nash, the Englishman who designed Regent's Park in London. The square was initially planned to be an elegant space with balconies overlooking the central area, but in a burst of utilitarianism lacking any aesthetics, they covered the area with an iron structure in 1914.

About Vocabulary
Molina Square got its name from this urban planner, who became the city's municipal architect from 1855 onwards.

Did you know?
La Boqueria is the biggest market in Spain, covering an area of 2,583 square metres.

SOME INFO

Some say that the beginning of flower sales on La Rambla was a custom followed by many market vendors: they often gave a flower as a gift to the customers with every purchase.

The Man Who Collected... Dead Animals

Legend has it that in the filthy streets of medieval Barcelona, there was a man dressed in a green cape, carrying the city coat of arms and a very loud bell. He was known as the *matxo de la gatera*, responsible for collecting dead dogs, cats, and other small animals within the city walls. These deceased animals had to be taken outside the city to prevent infections, and the hospital covered the cost of this service. The *matxo de la gatera* used to pull his cart himself or, if he was lucky, with the help of a horse.

The *matxo de la gatera's* cart.

A Church Built by Everyone

The only fully completed medieval Catalan church can be found in the former extramural neighbourhood of Vilanova de la Mar. It's a stunning example of Gothic architecture and considered one of the most beautiful ones in Barcelona, and as you're probably aware, it's Santa Maria del Mar. But here's something interesting: before they started building the church, they came to an unusual arrangement. They decided that the church would belong exclusively to the people from Ribera and Vilanova de la Mar. Everyone in those neighbourhoods contributed money and work to make it happen. So, in 1329, King Alfonso the Benign laid the first stone.

The Charm of the Straight Line

The exterior of the building is really quite simple and robust. It only has three facades because the fourth one was connected to the wall that surrounded the area. There aren't many decorations on the walls, just two doors called the Sombrerers' Milners' door and the Moreres' Mulberries' door. They added another door later on, called the Born door, at the back of the church. But the most eye-catching thing on the outside is the big gargoyles.

Inside, it's a different story. Even though there are three separate sections, they wanted it to feel like one big wide and open nave. The sanctuary is not fancy, but it has great acoustics. They've been using it for concerts for a long time, and they always sound amazing.

The one and only Santa Maria del Mar.

SOME INFO

The rose window of Santa Maria del Mar isn't the original one. It actually collapsed on Corpus Christi Day in 1428 because of a big earthquake, measuring eight on the Richter scale, and with its epicentre in the Pyrenees. When they were trying to move the Virgin from the building to the cathedral, dozens of people died. They rebuilt the rose window in a flamboyant style between 1459 and 1460 and replaced the damaged stained-glass windows.

Did you know?
In the novel *The Cathedral of the Sea*, Ildefonso Falcones talks a lot about how the workers from the port and the people who lived in the neighbourhood helped build the church. They took on different tasks and some even carried heavy stone blocks from Montjuïc on their backs. So, you could say this church is a really moving example of a group of people coming together to make something amazing in the history of Barcelona.

La Rambla: From Sewer to Backbone of Barcelona

Once upon a time, La Rambla, now one of the city's most emblematic streets, was nothing more than a stinky sewer. According to Jeroni Pujades' 17th-century chronicles, it was a Roman construction made of rough stones, where all sorts of unattractive things would flow through. Who would have thought that such a place would eventually become a posh street lined with luxurious establishments?

Over time, the sewer transformed into a stream that was redirected elsewhere when the 14th-century Raval wall was built. From the 14th to the 17th century, La Rambla experienced a religious building boom. Jesuits, Carmelites, Trinitarians, Augustinians, and others all found their homes along this street. But amidst all the spirituality, there was also space for secular structures like the General Study building and the Holy Cross Theatre.

However, the tide turned in 1835 when convents were set ablaze and religious properties were seized in the following year by Mendizábal. Many of these religious buildings

Different images of La Rambla through the ages, from when it was a stream until today.

were demolished as a result. To make matters worse, the walls surrounding the area were torn down in the 1850s. It's easy to imagine the multitude of solariums they planned to build there, but over time, residential buildings and impressive structures like Hotel Oriente, Gran Teatro del Liceu, Boqueria market, and Plaça Real took their place. They even moved plane trees from Dehesa de Girona Park to provide shade along the old sewer, which was slowly turning into a street. After all these changes, Rambla became a popular promenade for the people of Barcelona. They would sit and chat on stone benches called "canapés" or rented chairs. It all started on July 28, 1781, when they placed three hundred straw seats along the street. The Rambla was especially popular among the bourgeoisie of the time. As time passed, the styles of chairs and their prices changed. The initial seats cost a quarter coin, but by the early twentieth century, it was ten cents. However, nothing lasts forever, and when democracy was restored after Franco's dictatorship, the rental of chairs stopped, and public benches were installed instead.

About Vocabulary
Some people say that the stream running through La Rambla used to be called the *cagalell*, kind of like a sewer.

Canaletes: The Fountain That Makes You Return

Legend has it that when the walls were built, two towers were erected at the entrance of Santa Anna Street and Tallers Street, where the current Rambla is. These towers were called *Canaletes* because they had channels to prevent water from collecting at the base of the walls during rainy days. These channels drained into the main stream flowing down the Rambla.

There is historical evidence of a fountain in that spot dating back to the 16th century. It was known to draw water from the Montcada Mine, which was said to have a pleasant taste.

In the 19th century, when the city gates and walls were demolished, they replaced it with a small cast-iron fountain that served the same purpose. They even thought about pets and included a small drinking trough for dogs.

SOME INFO

Legend has it that if you want to ensure your return to Barcelona, you must drink water from the *Canaletes* fountain.

Did you know?
Selling flowers in La Rambla started way back in 1853, in those old-school cast-iron kiosks. Later on, they upgraded to fancy glass ones. Back in the 19th century, it was the only place in the city where you could buy flowers.

The First Tourists in Barcelona Didn't Wear Mexican Hats

According to a Catalan maritime legend, many of the men who sailed with Christopher Columbus to discover America were recruited in Plaza del Rei. Can you even imagine their reaction when someone suggested going on a voyage to an unknown land?

For a long time, people believed that the Catholic Monarchs welcomed Columbus on the steps of Plaza del Rei when he returned from his first voyage to America. But now they say it actually happened at the Sant Jeroni de la Murtra monastery in Badalona. Apparently, Ferdinand and Isabella decided to move there for a few days of rest after Ferdinand survived an assassination attempt.

Wherever the reception took place, one thing's for sure: Columbus came back with some American natives in his crew. Can you imagine what those Americans must have thought when they saw a completely different landscape from their own?

An engraving from the 19th century showing Columbus offering the newly discovered lands to the Catholic Monarchs.

When Jousts Were Trendy

Right behind Santa Maria del Mar, there's this promenade that's been super important to the people of Barcelona since the 14th century. El Born used to be this big square where all sorts of activities were held: jousting tournaments, parties like carnival, New Year's Eve, and San Juan celebrations. It didn't matter what they were celebrating, whether it was a royal baptism or Saint George's day, they'd do it in El Born. This place was one of the main market squares where business, serious stuff, and fun all mixed. But it wasn't always a happy place. The Inquisition picked the promenade to stage some of their *autos de fe* (acts of faith) - brutal public punishments, like burning heretics at the stake. There were at least three of these crazy events recorded: one in 1568, another the next year, and the last one in 1647.

Two pictures showing different views of the El Born promenade from different times.

About Vocabulary
According to Víctor Balaguer, El Born promenade was like the main square in Barcelona. Balaguer says the name comes from the word *borneja*, which means to turn, and it refers to cool public events like jousts, tournaments, challenges, and duels.

After the War of Succession, El Born became a silent reminder of Barcelona's defeat. During the fighting in 1706, they put up a monument there to commemorate when Carlos of Austria beat Felipe of Bourbon.

Obviously, he was overthrown after Felipe's victory. Felipe made sure to set up a platform to punish the "treacherous" clergy.

Did you know?
The Gothic Quarter in Barcelona is the biggest medieval district in all of Europe that's still around today.

How to Turn a Debt-Ridden Hospital into a Work of Art

Back in 1401, Martí the Humane was there when they laid the first stone for the Hospital of the Holy Cross on Carme Street, which is now the home of the Institut d'Estudis Catalans (Institute of Catalan Studies) and the Library of Catalonia.

Successive plagues and population growth of the century filled up their services to the point of being unsanitary. Since they couldn't expand the existing buildings due to overcrowding in the Raval, they had to build a new headquarters from scratch.

The Hospital That Added a Saint to Its Name

Under Lluís Domènech i Montaner's project, construction of the new hospital began in 1902 on Sant Antoni Maria Claret Street, but it took eighteen years to finally open its doors. The delay was caused by a lack of resources and conflicts arising from the administration's management model at the time. Eventually, with financial help from Pau Gil, a wealthy banker from Barcelona, the hospital was completed. It was inaugurated in 1930, and as a gesture of gratitude to the patron who made it all possible, they added "Sant Pau" to the original name, Hospital de la Santa Creu.

SOME INFO

The pavilions on the right were originally meant for men and were named after saints, while the ones on the left were for women and had names of saints or virgins. Additionally, the pavilions near the entrance were smaller than the ones farther away. This was done to prevent the perspective from fooling the observer's eye and blocking the view of the more distant pavilions.

On the left and on this page, two images of the Hospital de la Santa Creu and Sant Pau.

Did you know?
The Hospital de la Santa Creu y Sant Pau is one of the biggest examples of Catalan modernist architecture. Surprisingly, it has managed to maintain this style despite later renovations.

Ads for Brothels Targeting the Illiterate

Back in the 15th century, some brothels were allowed to operate. Besides the Raval area, there were probably pleasure houses along the Carassa route, close to Princessa Street. The street got its name from the *carassa* situated on one of its corners. And what's a *carassa*? Well, it's a carved face in stone on a wall.

The *carassa* was a clear signal that the building was a brothel.

While nowadays only a few people may recognize the significance of this discreet urban feature, everyone understood its meaning a few centuries ago. Female faces carved on the outside walls indicated the presence of a nearby brothel. This sign was particularly helpful for foreigners and those who couldn't read. Considering the high illiteracy rates for many centuries, symbols like this must have assisted more than a few people in finding what they were after.

The Counterfeit Coin Maker

Coins in Barcelona have been minted on and off since Roman times. However, starting from the 13th century, the minting activity became more consistent. The mint or coin factory of Barcelona was believed to be situated between La Seca, Cirera, Flassaders, and Mosques streets, at least since 1441. Unfortunately, the original building no longer exists, and the facade we see today is a reconstruction from the 18th century.

The entrance to the mint, that is the coin factory.

The Decree of the New Plant put an end to the production of coins labelled "Made in Barcelona" for a considerable period. However, during the French occupation in the early 19th century, the mint was revived, and coins were minted with the word *peseta* included in their design, marking a historic first.

Did you know?
A chimney was constructed in the mint during the late 19th century, and remarkably, it still stands today.

The guild of coiners was highly regulated, and one could only become a member through inheritance or by royal grace. In *Històries i llegendes de Barcelona* (Stories and Legends of Barcelona), Joan Amades recounts the tale of one of the most famous coin makers in the city's mint, Janet del Barretó. Rumor has it that Janet, not content with the limited profits from such a tightly controlled business, decided to make his own counterfeit coins in the hopes of finding better fortune with his new product. Unfortunately, luck was not on his side, and he was eventually discovered and imprisoned. The prison sentence was so lengthy that by the time Janet del Barretó was released he was already an old man. With nothing to do, the man who once tried to outsmart the Crown and make money, was now begging for handouts. The people in the neighbourhood took a liking to him and helped him out as much as they could. They said he was so skilled that he could even make fake coins using a simple orange peel.

About Vocabulary
The word *peseta* comes from the Catalan word for piece, *peça* or *peceta*. In the 15th century, some small silver coins started being called *pesetas* due to their size. The Catalan term eventually became the prevailing name for these coins throughout the country in 1868, thanks to the efforts of Laureà Figuerola, the Minister of Finance at the time.

Pesetas of the Second Republic.

If You Breastfeed, Don't Have Sex

During the Middle Ages, wealthy women used to hire wet nurses to breastfeed their newborns. Being a wet nurse was a well-paid job, and a contract had to be signed before a notary for each new child, ensuring that the nurse would provide services until the baby was old enough. If the nurse broke the contract and stopped breastfeeding before the agreed time, she would have to pay a hefty fine or face imprisonment. Additionally, while breastfeeding, wet nurses had to follow some strict rules, such as refraining from sexual activities. It was believed that if a woman got pregnant while breastfeeding, her milk would turn sour.

If someone needed to find wet nurses in Barcelona, they would go to La Flor de Lliri Street. In 1444, an inn with the same name as the street was established there. Coincidentally, many wet nurses from outside the city chose this inn to stay and advertise their services. Word quickly spread within the city walls, making this inn the go-to place for all those who needed the services of a wet nurse. Both the street and the inn ended up being called *las nodrizas* the wet nurses.

The Patron Saint of Wet Nurses

Saint Agatha is the patron saint of wet nurses. You can call on her when you're dealing with chest pains, tough childbirth, or issues with lactation. Back in the day, on February 5th, which was Saint Agatha's feast day, both wet nurses and mums with little ones would munch on a special sweet bun and wash it down with a glass of milk. The belief was that this treat would magically boost their milk supply.

Picture showing the Martyrdom of Saint Agatha.

Let me tell you a bit about Saint Agatha of Catania 231-251. She was a young woman who made a brave choice not to have sex with the Roman governor, Quincianus. Instead, she dedicated herself to Jesus' teachings and remained a virgin, committed to God. Well, the governor didn't take kindly to her rejection, so he ordered her to be tortured for being a Christian. They actually cut off her breasts, but Saint Peter worked his healing magic and made her wounds disappear. The governor then decided to sentence her to death by making her lie on a bed of burning coals. But guess what? An earthquake showed up, saved her from the fiery fate, and crushed the governor's head with a falling wall. Although she escaped her tragic destiny, poor Agatha didn't have a particularly joyful life. She ended up dying while locked away in a prison.

About Vocabulary

Oh, and speaking of wet nurses, did you know there used to be a job called *tirapits* or *xuclapits* "breast suckers" back in the day? These were women who were responsible for sucking on the breasts of wet nurses to keep the milk flowing smoothly.

Did you know?

The profession of wet nurse has been around since Roman times.

The Most Media-Savvy Bandit

In the ancient Sant Martí de Provençals district, there's this park called Guinardó Park. It got its name from a nearby farmhouse called Mas Guinardó, which belonged to the family of a famous bandit named Perot Rocaguinarda (1582-1635).

Engraving depicting Rocaguinarda and his bandits.

Rocaguinarda was the most infamous boss of Catalan bandits until 1611. He became so famous that even Miguel de Cervantes wrote about him in chapters sixty and sixty-one of the second part of Don Quixote. In those pages, the bandit hangs out with Don Quixote during his visit to Barcelona.

The Ghost Who Forgave Rocaguinarda's Sins

Barcelona street plaque honouring Perot Rocaguinarda.

Rocaguinarda was a true highway robber and became a legend in Catalan folklore. Here's a wild story: the priest at the Church of Pi made the mistake of celebrating Mass without an altar boy. Shortly after, he died, but his ghost couldn't rest in peace with a poorly conducted Eucharist in his resume. So, whenever someone entered the church, the ghost priest would show up and ask them to be his altar boy for a final Mass to redeem him from his sin. People freaked out and ran away from this house of God.

But one day, Perot Rocaguinarda walked into the church and, being fearless as always, agreed to help the tormented ghost. He played the role of an altar boy in a spooky Mass. And you know what? The grateful ghost thanked him and flew up towards heaven while telling the bandit that all his sins were forgiven. After being deeply affected by these events, Perot stopped stealing and headed to Sicily to join the Castilian troops. Rocaguinarda went from being a legendary figure to a mere mortal.

About Vocabulary
It is believed that the Catalan word *guinardó* comes from *guinarda*, which means fox in old Catalan. But different scholars have proposed various alternative explanations.

Did you know?
Mas Guinardó was bought by the Council in 1906 and currently serves as the central hub for district organizations.

SOME INFO

It is said that when Cervantes visited Barcelona, he stayed at number 2 Passeig de Colom. The house remains exactly as it was in the 16th century.

When Sending Letters Was a Luxury

In the olden days, if someone wanted to send a letter, they had to arrange a private contract and pay someone to deliver it. These messengers were known as *correos* (postmen), and they received different nicknames based on their mode of transportation. A postman who walked was called a *correo de alpargata* "espadrille postman," the fortunate one who rode a horse was a *correo de caballo* "horse postman," and those who sailed were referred to as *correo de mar* "sea postmen." As time passed, they started setting up routes. The postmaster was in charge of organising the postal service back then. He had to accommodate foreign messengers and their animals, and find available carriers when someone wanted to send something. The postmaster's house had to be well-equipped, with a decent stable, a room for travellers, and a reception area for customers. In Barcelona, the first recorded post office was located on the current Correu Vell (Old Post Office Street).

About Vocabulary
This thoroughfare used to be called Puiggener, named after a noble Barcelona family who had their palace at number 5. When the first mail service was inaugurated, the street became known as Estafeta. But when the service moved to a different location much later, it started being called Correu Vell Street.

Did you know?
The postal workers formed a guild in 1587.

Chapel of the Our Lady of Guia or of Marcus, on lower Sant Pere Street, in the Ribera neighbourhood.

SOME INFO

Before setting off on their journey, messengers had a tradition of stopping in front of the chapel of the Virgin of Guia or Marcús, located outside the walled area. There, a priest would bless them to ensure a safe journey.

The Owner and Lord of Montjuïc

Bernat Marcus was one of the few members of the bourgeoisie who got to join Count Ramon Berenguer IV's council even though he wasn't a noble. He may not have had fancy titles, but he had loads of money. He owned properties all over the city, especially up on Montjuïc mountain. With all that cash, Marcus was super active in politics, hanging out with Ramon Berenguer and Petronila. And when he wasn't busy with the count, he even had his own chapel built. By the way, he used that chapel to set up the first postal route in Europe, mostly for his fellow bourgeoisie.

He Who Calls for Bad Weather Without an Umbrella Will Surely Get Wet

Marcus must have been quite famous back in the day, because we've still got some legends about him. One of them says he owned this piece of land next to Santa Maria church. It was just sitting there, not being used for anything, and the priest of the church knew Marcus was loaded. So, he asked Marcus if he could turn it into a cemetery. Marcus thought it over for a bit and eventually said yes. But he had one condition: if nobody got buried there within two months, the land would go back to him. Sixty days went by, and wouldn't you know it, nobody died during that time. Marcus was over the moon with his luck, so he went to the church to claim what was rightfully his. What happened next was definitely wasn't part

Bernat Marcus has a little square near Princess Street dedicated to him.

of his plan. As he claimed what he thought was rightfully his, Marcus suddenly dropped dead on the spot. And just like that, the bourgeois became the first corpse laid to rest in the Fossar de les Moreres cemetery.

SOME INFO

Nobody knows for sure if Marcus actually owned the Fossar de les Moreres. What we do know is that in 1166, he donated land and money to build a cemetery for pilgrims and the poor near Princess Street. That's where you'll find the small square named after Marcus today.

The Last Kiss Before Dying

Carrer dels Petons (Street of Kisses).

It's said that those condemned to die had their final chance to bid farewell to their loved ones on a narrow street leading to Commerce Road. Once they passed this street, they were taken to the Ciutadella esplanade, where they were either hanged or, after the gallows were abolished, killed by garrote strangulation. This alley is known as the la carrer dels Petons (Street of Kisses).

About Vocabulary
This road used to be called Jaume Negre before, and later Fusina, referring to the area's depths.

La Mercè That Made a Thousand Locusts Disappear

Legend has it that on the night of September 24, 1218, the Virgin Mary appeared to James I, Pedro Nolasco, and Raymond of Penyafort. She came down to Earth to ask them to establish an order of monks tasked with rescuing imprisoned Christians by the Saracens in the Crusades. And they listened to her because it is said that this order, known as the Order of Our Lady of Mercy and the Redemption of Captives, would achieve the liberation of three hundred thousand prisoners.

With such an optimistic background, when Barcelona was attacked by a plague of locusts in 1687, the citizens thought of her. Therefore, they invoked her in search of a miracle for the city. And it seems that she listened to them, as the plague eventually disappeared. In gratitude, Barcelona appointed the Mare de Déu de la Mercè (Our Lady of Mercy) as its patron, a designation that the Papacy wouldn't confirm until 1886.

Our Lady of Mercy, presiding over the basilica. Below, giants parading on the 24th of September.

The Mercè festivities began to be celebrated for the first time in 1872 following an initiative by Francesc de Paula Rius i Taulet (1833-1889), mayor of Barcelona. In 1902, Francesc Cambó (1876-1947), at that time in charge of the festivities in the city council, turned this celebration into what we can see today. For this, he could count on the collaboration of Josep Puig i Cadafalch and other intellectuals of the time. The *gegants* (giants), which were already traditional in the area, the *castellers* (human towers), the *cabalgata* (parade), and the *sardana*, which became the national dance of Catalonia, were incorporated. During Franco's regime, La Mercè would be a simple religious festival until in 1977, the mayor of Barcelona, Josep Maria Socias 1937-2008, decided to resurrect Cambó's idea.

Did you know?
Our Lady of Mercy is the patron saint of the Diocese of Barcelona and the city. The day of her celebration is 24th September.

Kings, Theatre, and a Maze

El parc del Laberint d'Horta (Horta's Labyrinth Park) is one of the most surprising places in Barcelona. Next to the Collserola mountain range, it was designed in 1791 by the same owner of the grounds: Joan Antoni Desvalls i d'Ardena (1740-1820). Desvalls, with the help of the Italian architect Domenico Bagutti, created what would eventually become an exponent of the neoclassical garden of the 18th century.

Although the garden is full of small details and wonderful corners, its emblematic feature is the maze, which was also designed by Desvalls himself. Made with 750 metres of trimmed cypresses, the maze has a marble relief with the figures of Ariadne and Theseus at the entrance and a statue of Eros in the centre. Joan Antonio Desvalls was a descendant of an ancient family of warriors from the 15th century. His ancestors participated in episodes such as the defence of the Alhambra and the siege of Almería.

Whoever manages to reach the center of the Horta Labyrinth will be greeted with a delightful discovery: a marble sculpture of Eros.

Joan Maragall with Utrillo in the Laberint d'Horta, in 1898, when Iphigenia in Tauris was performed.

Leaving the struggle to one side, he devoted himself to science and became one of the most enlightened men in the city.

In this park, which had once been merely an idea in his head, splendid events would take place in honour of kings such as Carlos IV, Ferdinand VII, Alfonso XII, or Alfonso XIII. The enormous garden was also used for cultural purposes, with Joan Maragall himself as the protagonist. In 1898, for example, the poet staged Goethe's Iphigenia in Tauris, which would be one of the many performances of classical theatre versions he would undertake.

In 1908, another important event took place, when Alfonso XIII and other personalities attended a performance of William Shakespeare's A Midsummer Night's Dream. And with the commemoration of the centenary of Romanticism in 1930, all kinds of performances were staged in the Nymph's Grotto.

Did you know?
It's the oldest surviving garden in Barcelona.

SOME INFO

The park didn't open to the public until 1971, four years after the Desvalls family had handed it over to the city council.

Barcelona Embraces the Press

On 7th January 1762, some barber shops in Barcelona started selling the city's first newspaper. It was a publication directed by Pedro Ángel de Tarazona, a journalist and business agent from Navarre who had settled in the city. Trying to emulate the spirit of the *Diario Noticioso, Curioso-Erudito, Comercial, Público y Económico* sold in Madrid, Tarazona created the *Diario curioso, histórico, erudito y comercial*, público y económico. But the newspaper would only survive for fifty-three days.

The *Diario de Barcelona,* a title that would see the light thirty years later than Tarazona's fared significantly better and would remain in existence until 1993. Its founder, Pedro Pablo Husón de Lapezarán, was a Neapolitan who obtained a royal privilege from Carlos IV. He would be given exclusivity if he published the news and advertisements of his subscribers without charging them anything. And he did so for a long time.

El golpe de Estado

UN PARENTESIS DE ANSIEDAD

A page from the *Diario de Barcelona* from 1923.

A Palace Funded in the Americas

Since Columbus set foot in America, the kings had been very clear about the importance of maintaining those lands under Spanish dominion. That is why they always sent personalities to act as governors of the Crown in each of their acquisitions.

One of these characters was Felipe Manuel d'Amat (1707-1782), a Catalan military man who had been sent to America first as the governor of Chile and later with the title of viceroy of Peru. Cruel and viscerally racist, Amat mistreated the native Americans wherever he went. But he was also authoritarian with his own people, as well as corrupt with the Crown to which he owed loyalty: it turned out that neither all the coins, nor all the silver, nor all the gold that had ended up in his pocket were truly his.

In 1767, he bought plots of land on La Rambla to build a palace that he wouldn't see until 1777, when he returned from America at the age of seventy. Shortly thereafter, he married Maria Francesca Fivaller y Bru, a very discreet twenty-four-year-old girl whom people knew by the nickname of the *Virreina* (Vicereine) – the wife of a Viceroy.

Felipe Manuel d'Amat, better known as Viceroy Amat or Viceroy of Peru, a disloyal and cruel viceroy.

Whoever Does It, Sometimes Pays for It

Perhaps because Amat provided good services from America to the central government, the Crown looked the other way while he was in its service. After all, they must have thought, the man had faithfully defended Spanish power in his territories, harassed by the English and the French, in addition to maintaining sovereignty over the Falkland Islands and Cape Horn.

But his final years in Barcelona were difficult. The grateful Crown, however, didn't intend to forget about the viceroy's embezzlement, and during the few years that Amat lived in his dream palace, he was harassed by the courts day and night. Some believe that he ended up committing suicide, although this fact is not documented anywhere.

The Palau de la Virreina (Vicereine's Palace) was built in 1777.

Francesca Fivaller continued living in the palace until her death in 1791. The heirs sold the property to Josep Carreras d'Argerich in 1835, who installed the most comprehensive library in Barcelona. Over the years, the building was left abandoned until the city council purchased it in 1944, when it was almost in ruins. Today, fully restored, it serves as the headquarters of the Institute of Culture of the municipality, and its most spectacular halls are dedicated to temporary exhibitions.

Did you know?
The Palau de la Virreina is considered the finest example of Baroque applied to the civil architecture of Catalonia.

SOME INFO

The operetta *La Périchole*, by Jacques Offenbach, is inspired by the love story that the Viceroy had in Peru with a popular Peruvian actress known as *La Perricholi*. In 2003, the theatre company Dagoll Dagom brought their own version of the story to the stage.

Chamber Pots Behind the Doors

Years ago, it was customary to leave a chamber pot behind the door of each house. But when General Carlos de España (1775-1839) came to Barcelona in the service of Ferdinand VII, he didn't find this tradition to his liking. In fact, he found it so unpleasant that he requested that to be immediately discontinued.

In response to the new order, people rushed to remove the chamber pots from behind their doors. But as you know, it's difficult to break certain deeply rooted customs among the population. A wealthy gentleman on Mercaders Street was not quick enough in getting rid of his chamber pot, and as punishment, he had to stick his head inside a latrine for a whole day. Without doubt, a cruel and unusual punishment.

A Very Unlucky Opera House

The first building that would house the Gran Teatre del Liceu Liceu Opera House was erected on the orders of the merchant Joaquim de Gispert (1799-1862) on the site of an old Trinitarian convent dating back to 1662. Since it was built, the Trinitarian convent hadn't experienced many moments of peace. During the Napoleonic wars, it was used as a warehouse; later it would become the headquarters of a politically liberal club, and finally, it returned to its religious character. It is not known whether it was due to the burning of religious buildings in 1835 or one of Mendizábal's confiscations, but the building ended up in ruins and left a hole on La Rambla that was quickly filled again, replacing the religious with artists.

The theatre was inaugurated on April 4, 1847. But the Liceu would not enjoy tranquillity for, as in 1861, a large part of the building caught fire, most likely due to a poorly extinguished oil lamp. The reconstruction was carried out by Josep Oriol Mestres, who added a large rest hall and decorated the rooms and the ceiling of the central space with frescoes by the best Catalan painters of the 19th century. And all of this was accomplished in the record time of one year.

The Gran Teatre del Liceu (Liceu Opera House) in La Rambla.

In the 19th century, the theatre was not only used as a place to perform opera but also as a venue for social events such as carnival parties. Due to these gatherings, a portion of the more conservative and fearful sector of Barcelona society saw the theatre as an unacceptable centre of entertainment for Christian morality. If we add to this cheerful character of the theatre the incident of the fire, it's not surprising that rumours began to circulate in Barcelona about the existence of indignant spirits of the Trinitarian friars who had been buried in the convent and wanted to punish the Liceu.

The Anarchist Bombing of the Liceu

Le Petit Journal
SUPPLÉMENT ILLUSTRÉ
LA DYNAMITE EN ESPAGNE

On November 7, 1893, it would once again be a day of mourning for the Liceu. Santiago Salvador, a thirty-year-old anarchist, threw two Orsini bombs into the stalls of the theatre during the intermission of the performance of *Guillaume Tell* (William Tell). He wanted to avenge the murder of Paulí Pallàs, an anarchist who had attempted to assassinate the Captain General of Catalonia, Arsenio Martínez de Campos. One of the bombs caused around twenty deaths. The other one didn't explode because the skirt of one of the victims cushioned the blow. This unexploded device can be seen at the Barcelona City History Museum.

Salvador fled to Zaragoza, but a year later he found himself surrounded by the police in his apartment in the Aragonese

Front page of *Le Petit Journal* announcing the Liceu bombing. Below, Santiago Salvador and one of the bombs he used that didn't explode.

capital. The man shot himself in the chest, and while the police were breaking down the door, he also attempted to ingest poison. But his double suicide attempt failed, and after being treated in the prisoner's ward of the Hospital de Zaragoza, he was transferred to Barcelona to stand trial. The anarchist, realizing his end, wrote a letter to the judge declaring himself repentant and asking for forgiveness for what he had done. But there was no redemption for the anarchist, who was executed by garrotte on November 21, 1894, in Barcelona.

Did you know?
The Gran Teatre del Liceu is regarded as one of the most important opera houses in the world.

SOME INFO

Unlike other European cities, where the monarchy paid for the expenses that opera theatres might have, the Liceu had to be built through contributions from private shareholders. For this reason, it doesn't have a royal box.

A Square with Lanterns by Gaudí

Plaça Reial is the only square with arcades in the city. It was built in 1848 on the grounds of the Capuchin convent of Santa Madrona, which gives its name to this stretch of Las Ramblas. Designed by Francesc Daniel Molina, it's balanced, elegant, with

Lantern in Plaça Reial designed by Antoni Gaudí.

The Plaça Reial, one of the most emblematic in Barcelona, on a Sunday morning.

symmetrical lines and a taste in accordance with the European aesthetics of the 19th century. The Three Graces fountain in the centre of the square is accompanied by two lampposts that Gaudí designed in 1878 at the tender age of twenty-six.

Did you know?
The square is considered the first significant urban renewal project of 19th-century Barcelona.

About Vocabulary
The name of the square came from the desire to dedicate it to Fernando VII, as he was on the throne at that time. Against the backdrop of Spanish absolutism, everything was done to exalt the monarch.

SOME INFO

The square connects to the first covered passage built in Barcelona, the Bacardí passage.

An Impressive Palace for Catalan Music

Back in 1891, musician Lluís Millet and composer plus writer Amadeu Vives teamed up to start the Orfeó Català. Not long after, they hired one of the quintessential Modernist architects, Lluís Domènech i Muntaner, a local from Barcelona, to design their headquarters. Just like more than fifty years earlier with the Gran Teatre del Liceu, the funding came from Catalan industrialists and financiers. They bought this old spot where the San Francisco convent used to stand and started building in 1905. It was all set and done by 1908, and they opened the Palau de la Música Catalana on December 8, 1909.

Details of the Building

In one corner of the building, there's this fancy sculpture called *La cançó popular Catalana* by Miquel Blay. A female figure serves as the figurehead, and behind her, you have people from all walks of life, showing that this palace is for everyone. Above the crow, Sant Jordi (Saint George) crowns the scene.

The concert hall is lit up with colourful stained-glass windows that go from the floor to the ceiling on both sides. Right in the middle, there's a huge lamp that looks like an upside-down ball, shining like a big sun with golden crystals, and it's got blue and white crystals with ladies faces around it. On the left, there's a scene of Catalan folk music with a statue of Josep Anselm Clavé under a tree and a group of singers. The stage is like a semi-circle with 18 muses sculpted in mosaic, each one holding a different instrument.

Crystal chandelier and sculptural ensemble on the façade of the Palau.

SOME INFO

Pau Casals conducted the Orfeó orchestra from 1920 until 1936 when the Spanish Civil War broke out.

The Rebellion of the Palau Audience

Back in May 1960, when Franco decided to visit Barcelona, there was this show at the Palau de la Música where they wanted to perform the *Cant de la Senyera*. But guess what? They weren't allowed! The crowd wasn't having any of that. They got all riled up, stood their ground, and started belting out the anthem. Some brave activists even passed out flyers against the dictator. Jordi Pujol, who wasn't even there, got himself arrested for this whole ordeal and had to face a military court.

Did you know?
In 1971, the Palau de la Música was declared a National Monument, and in 1997, it was recognized as a World Heritage Site by UNESCO.

A Very Prestigious Brothel

There were all kinds of brothels on La Rambla and Raval. Some were dirty and dusty, while others were elegant and refined; Barcelona had options for every taste. Many of them welcomed concerned fathers who were worried about their sons' initiation rites. They would often take their young ones to a known and expensive prostitute to be taught the "art of love" without experiencing major traumas.

One of the top-notch brothels in the area was Madame Petit's, on Arc del Teatre Street. They had a crew of talented ladies who made quite a name for themselves but at the beginning of the 20th century, it went into decline. In the post-war period, the establishment was already quite run down, and society was very impoverished. Over the years, the once splendid brothel ended up becoming a cheap boarding house rented by the hour to the prostitutes of La Rambla.

Barça: Born out of Rejection

Official Crest of Football Club Barcelona.

The year is 1899, and a 22-year-old Swiss national named Hans Gamper sets foot in the city of Barcelona for the first time. In his own country, he is already known as one of the best football players in Switzerland. Active by nature, Gamper and a few friends tried to join Català FC, but they were turned down. Lacking success, they decided to start their own club.

In the same year he arrived in Barcelona, Gamper headed to the editorial office of the magazine *Els Sports*. He wanted to publish an advert for football enthusiasts to get in touch with him. From this call, and from the friendships he'd already made, Football Club Barcelona was born.

The place: 5, Montjuïc Street, in El Raval, headquarters of the Solè gymnasium. The day: 29th November. A story of passion had begun.

Did you know?
Gamper was part of the team until 1903 and was their first standout player, scoring 120 goals in 51 matches.

We Celebrate at Canaletes

The Canaletes fountain is the traditional celebration spot for Barça's victories. This tradition seems to have come from the custom started by the now-defunct newspaper *La Rambla*. Located across from Canaletes, the newspaper began writing breaking news on chalkboard placed on the street. Curious onlookers would stop to read the headlines and, if interested, might even buy a copy of the publication.

The newspaper's staff noticed that match results were what attracted the most occasional readers, and seeing that the initiative was quite successful, they continued to use the chalkboard.

Fans of the different teams would gather to talk and discuss the results. Over time, even though *Els Sports* eventually closed, the *culés* Barcelona fans continued to gather there following a Barça victory.

Gathering of culés (Barça fans) at Canaletes Fountain.

Once Upon a Time, There Was a Jordi Who Became a Saint

The festival of Sant Jordi (Saint George), on 23rd April, is one of the celebrations that encourages lots of people to take to the streets. But who was Sant Jordi?

We all know the legend of Sant Jordi and the dragon, and it has probably been handed down to us because the Archbishop of Genoa, Iacopo da Varazze Jacobus de Voragine (1230-1298/99), included it in his book *La leyenda sanctorum o Leyenda áurea* Readings of the Saints or The Golden Legend. This volume, filled with hagiographies, was one of the most widely known in medieval Europe. Perhaps that is why the story is also explained in places like England, Portugal, Greece, Hungary, Serbia, and Ethiopia.

A Roman Soldier Among the Christians

Jordi, from the Latin *Georgios*, means peasant. But etymologies aside, the boy didn't work the land; instead, he became a soldier and advisor to Diocletian, the greatest persecutor of Christians in history.

Jordi was born around 275 or 281 in Lod, a city near Tel Aviv. Following in his father's footsteps, he enlisted in the Roman army, where he served until the year 303 when Diocletian decided to wage his own war against the Christians. Seeing the emper-

Did you know?
Abbot Oliba 971-1046 consecrated an altar in honour of Sant Jordi in the monastery of Santa Maria de Ripoll.

or's plans, Jordi refused to persecute the Christians and claimed that he was one of them. In making this confession, the soldier knew he was condemning himself: he was tortured until he was finally beheaded on 23rd April of that same year. His body was buried in Diópolis, a Roman colony that had been established in his hometown.

When the Crusaders captured Diópolis in 1098, they discovered the story of Jordi and were greatly impressed. They spread the legend of the saint everywhere. The word of mouth became so widespread that the tale even reached Richard the Lionheart 1157-1199, who developed a strong devotion to the saint.

SOME INFO

The patronage of Sant Jordi in Catalan lands has been documented since the 15th century. The legend brought him to Catalonia to aid Catalan counts like Borrell II or James I in their multiple battles.

This depiction of Sant Jordi Saint George presides over the Palau de la Generalitat.

3. Curiosities of a Growing City: Industry, Business, Transportation

Urban Life in the Countryside

Until the 10th century, most of the residents of Barcelona worked in the countryside. The production from workshops, both inside and outside the city walls, was only intended for the local market. But with the gradual population growth, economic activity increased substantially, and new trades emerged.

❖ ❖ ❖

Looking Outside for What's Not Inside

The textile industry quickly distinguished itself among the guild industries.

About Vocabulary
During this period, the "domestic system" putting-out system was prevalent. This English expression refers to the rural workforce that, during less busy seasons, worked for wealthy artisans in the guilds. They received raw materials at home and, with the help of their families, produced goods from there.

In the 13th century, Barcelona became a major economic and commercial centre. Manufacturing production expanded remarkably. The textile sector, especially wool, stood out, benefiting from the royal decision to suspend the arrival of French fabrics following France's occupation of Sicily. The leather industry and shipbuilding in the royal shipyards were also important. However, the city's production capacity couldn't compare to other centres like Flanders or Italian republics. Therefore, many city merchants decided to to dedicate themselves to the re-export of products. Foreign items were bought to then resell them to other markets.

An Economy that Goes Up and Down

The union of Ferran of Aragon with Isabel of Castile not only marked the connection between the two crowns but also signified the beginning of a long journey through the desert of Barcelona, dragging the rest of Catalonia along the way. The War of the Reapers and the War of Succession represented an obstacle to the political, economic, and social evolution of the region.

Did you know?
During this time the guilds were born, which would always enjoy the support of public authorities.

Great Britain Determines Our Future

Barcelona remained primarily a guild city until the 18th century. But the rules of the international game changed. Great Britain had become wealthy through its colonies and controlled the seas. This provided it with low-cost raw materials and cheap labour. It lacked only one detail: an extensive market to sell its products. The country found itself with unstoppable production power, but protectionism, where all powers wanted to sell abroad and buy only at home, clipped its wings. The market had to be liberalised. Borders had to be opened.

It wasn't until the late 18th century when Barcelona, and Catalonia in general, began to experience an improvement both socially and economically. Progress had been made in agriculture, and the city had developed an emerging industry, although there was a need for marketing infrastructure to export products beyond the city walls.

Until the War of Succession, the only ones who could trade with the American colonies were the merchants of the Kingdom of Castile. Later, from Madrid, anyone who wanted to trade was allowed, regardless of their origin, to engage in trade with

Carlos III painted by the German artist Anton Raphael Mengs in 1762.

the other side of the Atlantic. There was only one condition: everything had to go through the port of Cadiz. The monarchs-imposed tariffs on the products that were exported and imported, and to keep the situation well under control, they centralised everything in this Andalusian port. Not only that, but the fear of English pirates prevented anyone from daring to sail alone. For safety, you had to travel in a fleet.

But the event that gave a decisive boost to Barcelona's trade took place in 1765, with a decree from Carlos III that allowed direct trade from several peninsular ports, including Barcelona, with some areas of the Caribbean. The possibility of trading with all of Spanish America came with the Free Trade Decree of 1778. Barcelona opened up to the world once again.

SOME INFO

One year before Carlos III's decree, in 1755, a group of Barcelona merchants founded the Barcelona Company of Trade in the Indies.

Did you know?

The gauge of Spanish railways was 1.67 millimetres longer than that of the rest of Europe's railways. This tiny snag, along with very strict tariff policies, hindered the growth of exports to Europe.

The First Modern Machines

One of the key factors that allowed for the rapid development of the industry in Barcelona was the constant technological innovation in the production processes, particularly in the textile world, and to a lesser extent, in metallurgy.

Driven by progress, Catalan entrepreneurs began by constructing water mills and introducing the first weaving machines. Later, manual spinning machines would follow. The goal was to create small and medium-sized companies that didn't require large initial investments. These new "capitalists" made the transition from the precarity of craftsmanship to wealth within one or two generations. They started as artisans, had relatively small workshops, paid low wages which the agricultural people were already used to, and, as they were used to saving and had frugal habits, they reinvested and grew. With this policy of living frugally, capital accumulated at a steady pace.

The Indian Fabrics

Felipe V had conquered Catalonia, but that didn't stop the entrepreneurial spirit in the Principality. Those engaged in trade with the Americas had saved money and soon found a good way to invest and make it grow. Thus, in 1737, the first Indian fabric factories were established in Barcelona. These businesses would form the foundation of the future Catalan textile industry.

The Indian fabrics were printed in Barcelona and sold in Europe.

Indian fabrics were ready-woven cotton textiles bought in India and here they were stamped with one or more colours on one side only. Once painted, the fabrics were called "Indianas" and were sold in Europe.

About Vocabulary

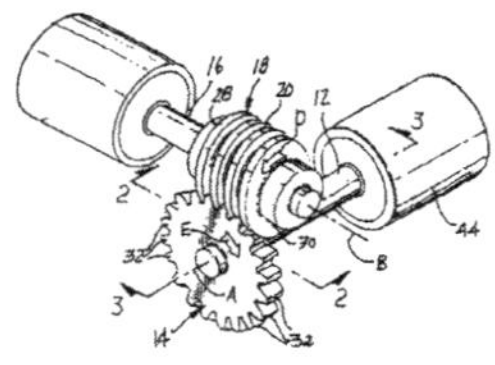

With this type of business, a new production system was introduced: manufacturing, which would become the precursor to the factory. For the first time, several dozen workers were gathered in the same space. The manufacturing plants were in an urban centre, and each one had an entrepreneur who organized and controlled production.

Joan Pau Canals' house in Barcelona, 1793.

An Ink Researcher

One of the pioneers of cotton factories in Barcelona was Esteve Canals. His son Joan Pau inherited the factory and, a chemist by profession, not only took care of the smooth operation of the business but also devoted some of his time to researching new methods for dyeing fabrics. His research led him to expand and improve the range of colours for fabrics and to extend the cultivation of red dye plants throughout Catalonia and Castile. This is a plant from which basic dyes are obtained and, because of how useful it was, would eventually be exported to the rest of Europe.

Did you know?
In 1772, Canals was one of the 25 founding manufacturers of the *Compañía de Hilados de Algodon* (Cotton Spinning Company) of Barcelona.

SOME INFO

Joan Pau Canals was a cultured man and had an extensive library. He taught courses at the Academy of Sciences and Arts of Barcelona and became a representative of the Catalan industrial bourgeoisie. He eventually would become the general director of the *Tintes de Reino* Dyes of the Kingdom and in 1780, he received the title of Baron of Vallroja, in reference to the cultivation he himself had popularized.

When Eating Chocolate Wasn't a Sin

One of the most exotic products that arrived from the American colonies was chocolate. Columbus had already brought cacao beans for the Catholic Monarchs, but since they didn't know what to do with them, they probably remained forgotten in some corner of the palace. To taste the sweet, one had to wait until the 18th century, when some Catalan friars who had settled in Mexico sent a shipment of cacao to the port of Barcelona, this time with the recipe that explained the steps to follow to make hot chocolate. Once in the peninsula, the friars who received the package prepared the chocolate, and its use gradually spread. But its popularity would grow thanks to a decision by the Church: eating chocolate did not break the fast. With such good publicity, this food soon became immensely popular.

Did you know?
In forty years, the number of chocolate makers in Barcelona multiplied by six.

The friars were responsible for the popularity that chocolate had in the 18th century. On the right, a mosaic from Petritxol Street, famous for its chocolate shops.

A Very Busy Port

When trade with America was liberalised, activity at the port of Barcelona increased considerably. The traffic of ships coming and going to the New World was relentless. They loaded oil, wine, and products such as fabrics, tools, tableware, furniture, and clothing. They departed for America and made stops at different ports where they sold all or some of their products and, at the same time, transported goods from one Latin American port to another.

The products they brought back to Barcelona were, basically, cocoa, coffee, cotton, sugar, and tobacco. From Barcelona, these goods

Castigo a un esclavo en Brasil (Punishment of a slave in Brazil), Jean-Baptiste Debret, 1802.

were distributed throughout Europe and in the domestic market. It was a smart business move: a commercial bridge had been created between Europe and America. The exchange of goods was transparent and yielded considerable profits. There was easy money changing hands in the form of fees and licenses, but alongside this business, another even more profitable exchange soon began to be practised: the slave trade. Many catalan, spanish, and european fortunes some still existing today grew thanks to this cruel stratagem.

Slavery also reached Barcelona

Some ships that set sail from Barcelona would "stop by" Africa to pick up slaves bound for the Americas.

Some of the ships that left the port of Barcelona, before heading straight to the Americas, would sail along the African coasts. There, they would contact local negotiators, who were often members of tribes that subjugated other tribes. The ships would load goods, fill their holds with Africans, and then disembark them on the American shores to deliver them to other negotiators, this time white ones. In America, the ships would load coffee, sugar, and tobacco and return with their holds filled with products they would later sell in Europe.

The English, Dutch, French, Portuguese, and Spanish were engaged in this trade for many years. Some Catalans followed this path with such enthusiasm that when slavery was abolished, it was hard for them to accept it. With the emergence of abolitionist laws in the last third of the 19th century, some Americans, Queen Isabella II of Spain, and anti-abolitionists, struggled to come to terms with it, among them a group of Catalan entrepreneurs and politicians rallied against it. In Barcelona, the reaction didn't take long, and the Anti-Abolitionist League was formed, with the support of the Bar Association and influential families deeply involved in the business.

SOME INFO

Around 1860, there were approximately ten thousand Catalans residing in Cuba. Most of them were engaged in trade, and many returned home with their pockets full. They were known as the *Indianos.*

Did you know?
In the 19th century, the number of African slaves forced to go to America amounted to seven million.

The Poverty of Progress

18th century Barcelona, once proud of its city walls and secure within them, had become too small. Demographic growth transformed the defensive wall into a suffocating barrier.

Barcelona couldn't expand horizontally, so it decided to reach for the skies. Floors were built upon floors, rooms were subdivided time and again until they became cramped spaces where tables, mattresses, and stoves shared the same area.

People used water from contaminated sources due to underground seepage from cesspools and the overloaded Barcelona sewer system, which only collected communal waste. Workers toiled in poorly ventilated and dimly lit factories. It is no surprise that cholera outbreaks, caused by food contamination and spread by flies, and cases of yellow fever, originating from tropical regions.

When Bread Was Worth Its Weight in Gold

In 1789, while Napoleon was starting his own revolution, Barcelona was immersed in a subsistence crisis. Workers' wages were low, and the prices of basic food items kept rising. The disarray in costs could have been influenced by the liberalization of the cereal trade and the disastrous harvests of recent years.

The working class in Barcelona had grown rapidly in a short time, and the struggle to find food every day was becoming more evident on many faces. Among those faces was Josepa Vilaret, known as "Negreta." Her husband worked as a domestic servant while she took care of their two children and worked odd jobs whenever she could find them.

On February 28th, after learning through a government decree that the price of bread was rising again and that, in addition, each loaf would now be smaller, Negreta joined a spontaneous revolt forming in the streets. Faced with the helplessness of not being able to afford the new prices, a group of angry women and men decided to express their frustration over the most basic of causes: hunger.

The Pla de la Palau around 1880.

The rebels began to gather on the streets until, towards the end of the evening, with their spirits agitated, some bread stalls like the one at *La Boqueria* caught fire. Faced with the chaos, the Captain General of Catalonia, Francisco González de Bassecourt, Count of El Asalto, deployed troops to the streets to quell the disturbance. But the protest didn't end there. The riots continued throughout the night, and the soldiers went back out into the streets, this time taking detainees to the police station.

Did you know?
The uprising began to take shape on the streets, and by the end of the evening, with emotions running high, some bread stalls, like the one in La Boquería, ended up being set on fire.

The following day, the spontaneous revolt shifted to *Pla de Palau* where, compelled by the situation, the government announced a reduction in the price of bread and the release of prisoners. The atmosphere didn't completely calm down because, in the afternoon, people began demanding price reductions for other items like oil, wine, and meat. The crowd headed back to Palau and encountered the cavalry. They threw stones and brandished sabres as the dead and wounded were left strewn across the street. By nightfall, groups of bourgeoisie, craftsmen, and nobles decided to patrol the streets to prevent further destruction.

On March 5th, with the city nearly calm, the search for the leaders of the revolt began. To make it more effective, a reward was offered to anyone who would give them information. Soon, there were over 40 detainees, including Josepa Vilaret, known as "La Negreta," who was said to have incited the crowd to revolt.

The government replaced the Captain General with Count de Lacy, a strong-handed man. He decided that six of the detainees would receive exemplary punishment: death. Guilds, prominent figures, and nobles from the city, bourgeoisie, and even members of the Church, pleaded for the punishment not to be carried out. However, the uprising needed to have a response strong enough to deter any further attempts to disrupt the social order.

Once at the gallows, Josepa was the first to die, perhaps because the Count of Lacy had publicly stated that he would not pardon her simply because she was a woman. The Negreta's body was buried, while the bodies of the five men were left exposed in different streets for a month and a half. That's how the Negreta died, after a day of anger upon realizing she couldn't afford bread for her children.

A Revolution in Gaseous State

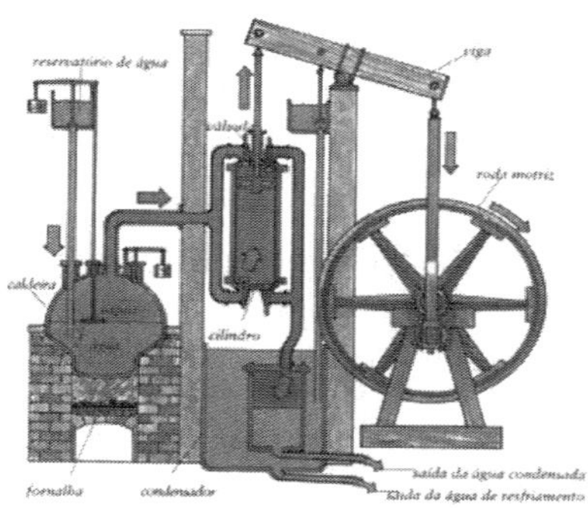

Above, workers of the Bonaplata factory, the first in Catalonia to install the steam engine, the most revolutionary invention of the time.

When the domestic system was reduced to a minimum, many people were forced to move to the big city. Barcelona's population grew exponentially: while at the beginning of the 18th century it had 30,000 inhabitants, by the end of the same century, it would host 93,000. A growth of 300%.

Although by the close of the century, Barcelona had not yet industrialized in all sectors, the city already had a capitalist mentality. The definitive leap came in the 1830s when the Bonaplata factory installed the first steam engine. This new invention would lead to a complete transformation of the city's production model. From now on, Catalonia, with Barcelona at the forefront, would become "the workshop of Spain."

Crazy Growth

The old textile factories of the 18th century multiplied. Between the thirties and forties, there were 240 Indian cotton factories, 524 silk weaving looms, and 2,700 ribbon and trim looms in Barcelona. Industries like embroidery, hats, and woollen textiles also grew exponentially. In 1863, the textile sector employed 17,231 workers, while the garment sector had 5,085. The rapidly developing sector was joined by industrial equipment factories, which were also growing at a good pace.

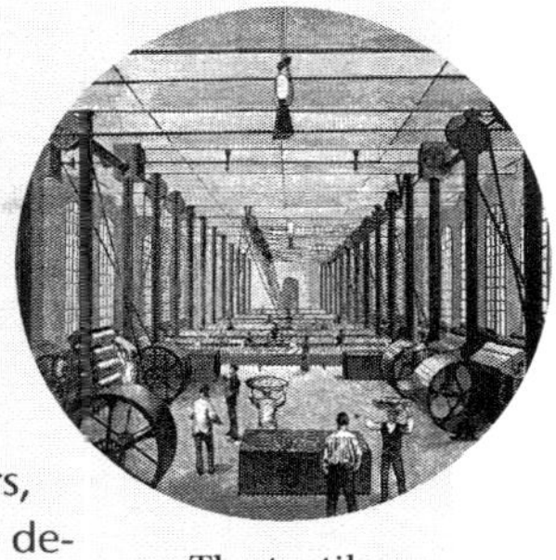

The textile industry kept growing and growing.

Beyond Fabrics

Some entrepreneurs wanted to open new markets and venture into industries other than textiles. However, Catalonia faced a disadvantage: the country suffered from a shortage of high-quality iron ore and coal. Nevertheless, companies like Nueva Vulcano foundry and La Maquinista Terrestre y Marítima emerged. The latter, founded in 1855 by Joan Güell, specialised in metal casting and the construction of railway equipment. Although metallurgy played a significant role in the naval manufacturing along the Catalan coast, it experienced a rapid decline due to the lack of raw materials. It was cheaper to buy from outside than to manufacture here, and there was little to debate about this.

SOME INFO

In the second half of the 19th century, Barcelona was the only city in Spain with a public engineering school.

The Most Powerful Conglomerate of the 19th Century

Three names stood out in the economic, industrial, and financial movement of the era: Joan Güell, Manuel Girona, and Antonio López y López, three entrepreneurs who united their interests, friends, family, and fortunes. They all knew how to surround themselves with a veritable network of collaborators, authorities, and influential acquaintances. They didn't just cultivate local connections; they managed to maintain excellent contacts, even with the monarchy. Güell, Girona, and López were the leaders of government protectionism and formed the largest financial core in Barcelona. Let's briefly review the history of these families.

The Güell Saga: Between Business and Art

The Vapor Vell factory, in the Sants neighbourhood, has been transformed into a state school.

The first of the Güell family to amass wealth was Joan Güell y Ferrer (1800-1872), who had successfully ventured to the Americas. Before returning from Cuba with deep pockets, Joan traveled through the United States and Europe for a while to study the latest textile innovations. Thus, the entrepreneur arrived in Barcelona equipped with a dual strength: money and knowledge. Armed with these two powerful tools, Güell established a textile factory in the Sants neighborhood. It was called El Vapor Vell, and by 1840, it already had 114 looms for fine fabric and 175 for cotton velvet and corduroy, all powered by steam. In 1851, the factory provided employment for 360 people.

After being widowed twice, Joan devoted himself wholeheartedly to business. Convinced that local production was more cost-effective than importing, he launched *La Maquinista Terrestre y Maríti-*

ma, dedicated to heavy machinery construction. Later, he became the director of *La Caixa d'Estalvis i Pensions de Barcelona*. Amidst all these business ventures, he found time to serve as a city councillor in the Barcelona City Council and a deputy in the Spanish Cortes. He was a committed protectionist and monopolist, and before his death, he amassed one of the largest fortunes of his time.

Eusebi Güell, businessman, industrialist, and economist, but better known for being the patron of Antoni Gaudí photo below.

The Son: Art and Business

Joan's heir, Eusebi Güell i Bacigalupi (1846-1919), received two-thirds of his father's fortune. With such a position, Eusebi was able to spend his youth educating himself and travelling. He lived in France and England, where he learned languages and, in the process, adopted bourgeois manners. His passions included architecture and art, politics, history, poetry, and theology. Like his father, Eusebi understood the economic reality around him and could spot the trends that would most benefit his interests. With such a clear business vision, Güell managed to give the family fortune a new boost.

In addition to his main company, *Güell Parelladas*, Eusebi participated in almost every sector of Catalan industry and finance: ships, railways, steel, gas, cement with the founding of the General Asphalt Company and Portland Asland, *la Caixa*, and the *Banco Hispano Colonial* (1876). As if that weren't enough, he also owned flour mills and bakeries, entered the wine sector, and served as one of the directors of the Felipepine Tobacco Company. Following in his father's footsteps, Eusebi also found time for politics. He was a city councillor in Barcelona, a provincial deputy, and a senator in Spain.

Two works endorsed by their patron: the Palau Güell and the Güell Crypt.

Gaudí's Great Friend

Eusebi Güell is known for his great business acumen, but he is best known for his role as a patron of Antoni Gaudí. Thanks to him, the architect was able to freely unleash his genius. Gaudí and Güell shared a personal friendship where money was never the topic of conversation. Art and a unique sense of spirituality bound them to such an extent that many of their contemporaries whispered that Eusebi was squandering his father's fortune by excessively funding Gaudí's works. However, this was not the case, as Güell's son would go on to die as one of the wealthiest men in Barcelona.

Did you know?
Eusebi Güell was also an active promoter of Catalan culture and, among other actions, supported the Floral Games and was the president of the Catalan Center.

SOME INFO

In 1908, Alfonso XIII, prolific in expanding the country's noble class, granted Eusebi the title of Count of Güell.

López y López, the Master of Maritime Transportation

Antonio López y López (1817-1883) was, undoubtedly, one of the first three residents of Barcelona to grasp the concept of a multinational company in Spain. Antonio was a young Cantabrian with limited resources. Pursuing the dream of the Americas, he emigrated to Cuba, where he eventually established a maritime route between Santiago and Guantánamo. With this business, his fortune grew considerably in a very short time. In 1853, he returned to Barcelona and began a series of contacts and investments that would make him one of the richest men in Spain in record time.

Antonio López y López.

His first venture in the Catalan capital was the steamship company Antonio López y Compañía, which he founded with two partners. Their ships connected Alicante, Valencia, Barcelona, and Marseille. In 1860, he used his infrastructure to transport troops and supplies to the colonies in Morocco. Shortly after, the royal house granted him exclusive rights to passenger transport between Spain and the Antilles. López had not forgotten his overseas experience and had enough foresight to understand that communication not just exports and trade was a strategic challenge for the time. In no time, he became the leading transporter in the country. Just with that, he made an immense fortune.

An Insurance that Spares You from War

In 1868, in Cuba, the first movement to achieve independence from the Spanish Crown began. This revolt would eventually become known as the Ten Years' War, Spain had significant in-

Engraving depicting the Ten Years' War.

terests in the battle because the country was on the verge of losing a valuable market: a massive source of raw materials and cheap labour. That's why the leaders didn't hesitate to burden the government's coffers in exchange for financing the expenses of the battle.

Driven by the situation in the Caribbean, López decided to establish an insurance company which citizens from across the state could turn to purchase personal insurance allowing them to avoid military enrolment. But the Cantabrian would still make more profit from the situation with the creation of the Hispano Colonial Bank. This was an institution formed with other Catalan and Cuban financiers who wanted to assist the government in financing the extraordinary expenses caused by the Ten Years' War. When the conflict ended in 1878, the entity

Catalan volunteers boarding for the Cuban War, from Barcelona in 1870.

transformed back into a traditional-style bank. The company would become the second major financial institution of the period, only behind "la Caixa."

In 1880, López restructured his initial shipping company and turned it into the Transatlantic Company. With his usual partners, he created the General Tobacco Company of the Philippines. Soon, they opened routes to Veracruz, New York, and the Río de la Plata. His economic empire had expanded in an unimaginable way.

Did you know?
He was a close friend of Alfonso XII, and in 1878, he was appointed Marquis of Comillas.

About Vocabulary
The monument to López in Barcelona was popularly known as the one of Black Sunday. Pulled down in 1936, it was reinstated after 1939.

SOME INFO

With a controversial personality, López's brother-in-law, Francesc Bru, carried out a fierce campaign against him by publishing *The True Life of Antonio López y López* (1885). In the book, he attributed the considerable fortune of the businessman to opportunism, the slave trade, deception, and cruelty.

The Son Who Did His Homework

Antonio López died suddenly in 1883. His son, Claudio López Bru (1853-1925), inherited the companies. Just as Eusebi Güell had done, the heir to the other economic giant in Barcelona created a network of companies that fed into each other. This way, he managed to save on external contracts for the shipping company, such as coal purchases. He established companies in Africa, Asia, and Oceania with a multitude of different but complementary industries in addition to new transportation lines. And that's how he transported thousands of immigrants to their

American destinations, some of whom, undoubtedly, dreamed of becoming another López and López.

SOME INFO

There is an open cause for beatification of Claudio López Bru. With his father, they founded a seminary for humble people that would eventually become the Pontifical University of Comillas.

Manuel Girona, the Man Who Collected Banking Entities

Manuel Girona (1818-1905) was the son of a small banker from Tárrega. Married to Carolina Vidal, the daughter of a financier, he expanded his father's fortune with a capitalist vision. One of the highlights of his success was the establishment of the *Banc de Barcelona* in 1844, the first private Spanish bank.

Later, with Güell and López, he founded the *Banco Hispano Colonial* and the *Compañía de Tabacos de Filipinas*. He also created the *Banco Hipotecario de España* and played a pivotal role in the creation of the Barcelona Chamber of Commerce, of which he was the president. He served as the mayor of the city, a conservative deputy, and a senator. Spanish President, Antonio Cánovas del Castillo (1828-1897) offered him the Ministry of Finance three times, though he never accepted the position. He also had the opportunity of being awarded the noble title of Marquess of Llano de Barcelona but declined it.

Girona supported the creation of a central bank responsible for issuing banknotes and operating throughout the entire national territory through a federated and decentralized system. He also advocated for state investment in public infrastructure and, when the state couldn't do so he believed private financing should be

The facade of the cathedral around 1880, before the works financed by Manuel Girona began.

allowed or made easier. This was consistent with his beliefs, as he also contributed to the funding of the *Gran Teatre del Liceu*, the University of Barcelona, the railway network, the port, and the 1888 Universal Exhibition of which he was the commissioner. He also took on full financial responsibility for the construction of the cathedral's facade. For centuries, the church had displayed a miserable brick wall as its front. In 1882, Girona made the decision to cover all necessary expenses. There were exactly six years left until the 1888 Universal Exhibition, and they needed to give a face to the city's most important temple.

It is said that the man was so mean that when one of his workers asked him for money for dentures, Girona replied that he didn't believe he had the right to change the designs of nature, which had intended him to be toothless.

SOME INFO

His body is buried in the cloister of the Cathedral of Barcelona.

Did you know?
Initially, the Bank of Barcelona had the exclusive legal privilege of issuing banknotes in the city. However, this situation only lasted until 1874 when the monopoly was granted to the Bank of Spain.

With Capitalism, The Proletariat Arises

The labour movement in Spain was born in Barcelona. Due to the high level of industrial concentration in the city, the Barcelona proletariat saw the need to adopt forms of organisation. From spontaneous riots or those incited by political agitators without specific goals, the transition throughout the century led to the creation of organisations.

In Catalonia, we can begin to speak of a labour movement starting from the year 1840. The workers were fed up with the misery imposed on them by meagre wages and the abysmal working conditions offered by employers. Furthermore, the gradual introduction of mechanisation provoked the anger of the workers, who saw it as a destabilising factor: it reduced the demand for labour and, therefore, contributed to job losses. The most significant clash of the mechanicalistic labour movement took place at the *Bonaplata* factory in August 1835, when the workers set fire to almost all of its facilities.

The workers burn down the Bonaplata factory, engraving from 1835.

In such a tumultuous time in the factories, advances in workers' rights were achieved through struggles. Only when a government with liberal tendencies oversaw the country did workers manage to take a step forward in improving their lot. Amidst all this give and take, in the early 1840s, the Mutual Association of Cotton Industry Workers was founded in Barcelona, eventually spreading throughout the Principality. Led by Joan Muns, the primary leader of the first Catalan labour movement, workers from other industries like shoemaking and woodworking also joined. The association even established an initial cooperative, the Fabril Company, and a joint commission with the employers.

The First Uprisings against Capital

General Prim

The tradition of free-thinking, active, and fighting Gràcia dates back to the events of 1870. At that time, General Joan Prim (1814-1870) was the president of the council of ministers of the central government and had just decided to send Catalan soldiers to the war in Cuba. Spain was afraid of losing the colony, and whatever it took to maintain Caribbean dominance was deemed necessary.

In response to this national demand, some residents of Gràcia took to the streets to protest. They refused to enlist their young people in a colonial war that only benefited industrialists and the capital. But the army arrived in the neighbourhood to carry out conscription. Nervous about the situation, the neighbours decided to ring the bell, which was located in the current Rius i Taulet square, to call the *somatén* local militia of Gràcia. Following the call of the bells, most of the town rose up and decided to confront the soldiers.

Tensions escalated, and the town hall ended up in flames. The army surrounded the town and besieged it for six days, ultimately choosing to quell the rebellion with bombs. The explosions left a river of blood with around thirty civilians dead and over a hundred injured. From this event, the Gràcia bell became a symbol of popular resistance. It also became the name of a widely read weekly newspaper until the early 20th century. Since 1870, revolutionaries have been accustomed to gathering in Rius i Taulet square, where the tower with its bell still stands. Can you hear how it sounds?

The bell of the "revolutionary" Rius i Taulet square.

And Then There Was Light... Electric. "The Canadian" Settles In Barcelona

The drive and entrepreneurial spirit of the early industrialists in Barcelona had their followers. Electricity had arrived in the city in 1882 for the benefit of a few streets and a handful of factories. Although the first power plant in Spain would be established just a year later Mata Street, near Paral·lel, it was clear from the beginning that it was insufficient.

Copy of a share in La Canadenca.

The city needed more electrical energy if it wanted to continue its development. This is when industrial engineers Carles Emili Montañès (1878-1974) and Fred Stark Pearson (1861-1915) came into action with the creation of the Barcelona Traction, Light and Power Company, a company headquartered in Toronto but known here by the nickname *La Canadenca* (The Canadian).

Pearson, a Canadian by birth, already had an impressive track record in the electrical sector: in addition to a hydroelectric plant at Niagara Falls, he had been involved with the Mexican Traction and the Brazilian Traction. Meanwhile, Montañès had contacts in Barcelona, a city untouched in the field of electricity where everything was yet to be done. With such a promising combination, the project was ambitious: to illuminate all of Barcelona with artificial light.

Fred Stark Pearson

Pearson and Montañès never hid their goal: they wanted to control the production, distribution, and consumption of energy in the area. Therefore, it's not surprising that *La Canadenca* acquired *Tramways de Barcelona* and the *Compañía Barcelonesa de Electricidad* (Barcelona Electricity Company) in 1912. The plan unfolded as

The three famous chimneys of *La Canadenca* that are still preserved on Paral·lel.

planned and received new contributions from Catalan figures like the industrial engineer and politician Ferran Fabra i Puig (1866-1944). But an event with global consequences would disrupt such spectacular growth: World War I.

Due to the conflict, the United Kingdom imposed restrictions on the outflow of money, and the two engineers found themselves without funding or a supply of raw materials to continue their project. The company was sinking, and Pearson, desperate, searched for alternatives. On a trip from New York to London, the ship he was travelling on, the Lusitania, was attacked by a German submarine with such bad luck that the businessman died in the shipwreck. Disaster loomed on the horizon. But Emili Montañès was used to difficult challenges and devoted all his efforts to ensuring that the existing power plants provided enough energy to keep Catalan industry running. Thanks to Spain's neutral position during the war, the country enjoyed a prosperous economic period, and *La Canadenca* was able to sell products throughout Europe.

Finally, in the final years of the 1940s, as a result of events that fatally wounded Catalan industry and plunged households into a subsistence economy, the company was forced to close. The government auctioned it off and handed it over to the company *Fuerzas Eléctricas de Cataluña SA* FECSA for 0.1% of its value, a blatant act of nepotism on Franco's part as a token of gratitude to the Mallorcan financier Joan March, who became the company's president. By the end of the 1960s, the Paral·lel power plant had closed. However, its three chimneys still stand tall, like three sentinels that haven't forgotten the passage of time in early 20th-century Barcelona.

SOME INFO

Fabra i Puig, who had been the mayor of Barcelona before Primo de Rivera's coup, gave the Fabra Observatory to the Academy of Sciences of Barcelona.

The First Electric Streetlights

Two of the public spaces that saw artificial light for the first time in Barcelona were the Pla del Palau esplanade and the Plaça Reial square, where some of the city's first streetlights were installed in 1890. It's worth noting the ones in Plaça Reial because they were designed by a very young Antoni Gaudí. Made of wrought iron, there are still written documents where the architect detailed the original colours with which he conceived the fixtures known as candelabras. These pleased the citizens because they were placed in areas not inhabited by the bourgeoisie, who were influenced by the classical taste of the era.

Electric streetlamp with modernist inspiration in Plaça Reial Royal Square.

The streetlights by Pere Falqués on Passeig de Gràcia didn't receive such a warm reception. Situated near the Arc de Triomf for the Universal Exhibition of 1888, these streetlights had a large bench at their feet. The intellectuals of the *noucentista* Catalan cultural movement era considered them to be hideous and absurd.

Did you know?
From this era there are also the lampposts that can be found today on Gaudí Avenue previously located in the current Joan Carles I Square and on Lluís Companys Promenade.

The Working-Class Consequences of the Universal Exhibition

The Universal Exhibition of 1888 had unexpected consequences for its organisers. Politically, on the one hand, it was an example of collusion between the monarchy and the Catalan bourgeoisie, but on the other hand, it acted as a trigger for the labour movement's activity.

The construction fever of the Eixample, and later the exhibition, had attracted people from all over Spain in search of work. Thus, the urgencies stemming from the project, the concentration of workers from various trades, and the ideas of the labour movements that were beginning to be heard throughout Europe created the perfect conditions for two events to occur in Barcelona that would have enormous consequences in the country's history. In August 1888, during the Exhibition celebration, the *Union General de Trabajadores* UGT trade union was founded, and shortly after, the Spanish Socialist Workers' Party PSOE held its first congress in Barcelona.

Pablo Iglesias, founder of PSOE.

SOME INFO

While all of this was happening, Republicans and Catalan nationalists led by Valentí Almirall protested against the implicit pact between the Catalan bourgeoisie and the monarchy.

The Grand International Hotel, designed by Domènec i Montaner, was built in 53 days for the Universal Exhibition of 1888 and knocked down once it was finished.

Skyrocketing Prices

The Universal Exhibition of 1888 caused significant price inflation. Taking note of this situation, the newspaper *La Vanguardia* published an article entitled "On the Occasion of the Universal Exhibition". The piece read as follows: "Barcelona is becoming impossible. Under the pretext of the exhibition, prices of things are skyrocketing and the fees for services are rising... barbers are charging an extra five cents for a shave, meat prices have gone up by ten, and carriage drivers are demanding sixty *duros* for each evening of racing; the only thing going down with all these increases is our wallets, which have long been dragging along the ground...".

A Union for All Workers

The *Confederación Nacional del Trabajo* CNT trade union and the *Federación Anarquista Ibérica* FAI association became so strong in Barcelona that their role would become decisive in the rifts that marked the Republican side during the Civil War. The CNT, established in Barcelona in 1911, would contribute to a very significant idea for the labour movement: the single union. Until that moment, unions had grouped workers of the same trade all together, but the CNT brought together all workers regardless of the industry they belonged to. The strikes of the second decade of the 20th century would show that this idea helped in terms of flexibility when it came to organising.

On the other hand, in 1927, the FAI wanted to bring together all anarchist groups in the Iberian Peninsula. Their purpose was to ensure the anarchist nature of the CNT and distance it from any understanding with political republican groups. However, during the dictatorship of Primo de Rivera, the FAI sided with left-wing politicians. Although it operated irregularly in its early years, it eventually gained significant influence.

The CNT was founded in Barcelona in 1911.

Did you know?
On July 19, 1936, the bar turned into a field hospital after workers and citizens stormed the military facilities of the Drassanes and the Government Military building, located between Anselm Clavé Street and Passeig de Colom. Throughout the war, *La Tranquilidad* continued with the spirit it had maintained up to that moment.

The Heart of La Tranquilidad Tranquility

La Tranquilidad was a bar that did little justice to its name: naturally noisy, the place was highly regarded by the politically engaged working class. It was a hub of revolutionary ideas, and although members of the CNT were the majority in the environment, there were also other sectors of the left. Opened in 1901 on Paral·lel Street at another location, it eventually moved next to the Victòria theatre at number 69. Nearby, on Mata Street, stood the Barcelona Traction, Light and Power Company, better known as *La Canadenca*, which began operating as the labour movement was starting to organise. The raw material for discussion was readily available.

The Strike that Established the Eight-Hour Working Day

In February 1919, a massive mobilisation began in the *La Canadenca* electric power plants as a result of a call by the CNT to prevent the dismissal of around a hundred employees. The rest of the electricity sector, along with the gas division, joined the protest. Before long, the city would be without electrical power, leading to the disruption of most transportation and industries in Barcelona, not to mention the complete suspension of supply to streets, businesses, and homes.

The 1919 protest began at La Canadenca (The Canadian).

In response to this situation, the government of Álvaro Figueroa, Count of Romanones (1863-1950), ordered the army to take control of the companies to restore electricity. The president also declared a state of war, and about three thousand workers were arrested. In reaction, other labour sectors joined the strike, which in Barcelona turned into a general one. The CNT controlled the strikers through vigilante groups to prevent excesses and took care to dispel rumours that could harm the protest.

Representatives of *La Canadenca* met with the government envoy and reached an agreement: the detained strikers would be released, *La Canadenca* would rehire all the workers, there would be a general wage increase, and the workday would be reduced to eight hours a day. To sign this agreement, after thirty-four days of strike, the CNT called an assembly in Les Arenes Square attended by more than twenty thousand workers. Salvador Seguí, *El Noi del Sucre,* tried to calm the situation and urged the workers to return to work because the agreement was

Salvador Seguí, *El Noi del Sucre.*

Workers derailing a tram during the general strike in Barcelona in March 1919.

Did you know?
This was the most significant strike Barcelona experienced in the years leading up to the Civil War.

reasonable. After 44 days of strike, the company had fulfilled its part of the agreement, and the workers returned to the factory. However, the military did not want to release 79 of the detained individuals. As a form of pressure, a new general strike erupted throughout the Principality on March 24th. Miguel Burgos, the secretary of the electricity sector of the CNT, died at the hands of the police. He became the first victim of the so-called "law of escapes." A state of war was declared, and the strike came to a halt. Carles Emili Montañès, who had been appointed as the civil governor due to his role in founding *La Canadenca*, resigned. The Count of Romanones would also have to do the same. Finally, the prisoners were released, and Spain became the first European country to establish an eight-hour working day.

One Against the Other: The Years of Gunmen

Unionism was becoming increasingly annoying for the employers and government officials.

Between 1916 and 1923, a hidden war raged in Barcelona. The victims could be both workers and employers or members of the public law enforcement forces. The CNT National Confederation of Labour had gained significant strength and was rapidly gaining supporters, especially in the aftermath of major strikes. Faced with such union membership, the Employers' Federation decided to take an extreme stance, eventually resorting to hiring hitmen to assassinate the most troublesome activists of the CNT. During this period, these hired gunmen enjoyed the unspoken approval of the authorities and the financial backing of industrialists. The hitmen, initially led by Police Commissioner Manuel Bravo Portillo and later by Baron de König, operated with impunity and, on occasion, attempted to blackmail members of the employers' federation.

The "Law Of Escapes" or How to Murder Someone and Make It Look Like Self-Defense

Severiano Martínez Anido, civil governor and murderer.

The police and the civil governor of Barcelona, Severiano Martínez Anido, practised what would later be known as the "law of escapes" during the years of workers' repression. The method was simple: the detainee was taken to a remote location and told to head towards a specific point or be set free. When the prisoner turned to leave, the police would shoot them in the back. The next day, it would be announced that the detainee had died at the hands of the public law enforcement services while attempting to escape. The first murder of this kind was that of Miguel Burgos, an electric sector CNT member, after the *La Canadenca* strike had already ended. In the same location, in the vicinity of the Arc de Triomf, and because of the "ley de fugas" (escape law), at least four more unionists would also lose their lives. The application of the escape law would peak in the assassination attempt on the labor leader Ángel Pestaña during his participation in a rally in Manresa. Both the chief of police in Barcelona and Martinez Anido were removed from their positions.

A Union in The Service of The Master

The Free Unions had emerged in 1919 as a breakaway faction from the CNT. The employers knew how to play their cards and used this organization to divide the CNT and assassinate its most renowned leaders, although the Free Unions often claimed their independence. However, they soon became the armed wing of the employers.

The Beginning of a River of Blood

Francesc Layret had been one of the most active lawyers defending the imprisoned workers during the *La Canadenca* strike. One year after that mobilization, the civil governor of Barcelona, Martínez Anido, had ordered a mass arrest of CNT militants. Among the detainees were Lluís Companys and Salvador Seguí himself, a friend of Layret. On November 30, 1920, as he left his home to attend to the defence of the detainees, a group of unknown as-

In the illustration above, the news reports the assassination of Salvador Seguí. Below, the funeral of Francesc Layret.

sailants fired several shots at him. The culprits were never found. His death would be the first of many that would occur in the following years, the years of the so-called social war.

The Dressmaker who Manufactured Bombs

Alongside the conciliatory politics of CNT members like Salvador Seguí, there was another anarchist tendency seeking answers through terrorist actions. At the beginning of the 20th century, there was a dressmaking workshop at number 10 Toledo Street. This wasn't unusual, as there were many such workshops in the city during those years. What wasn't quite so normal was what hid behind fabrics, scissors, and needles: an explosives factory. The owners of the place, Vicenç Sales and his partner Roser Benavent, were members of a highly active group that, in addition to holding meetings, manufactured their own bombs. Apart from the shop, they also had other clandestine locations where they would often take refuge from the hired gunmen of the employers.

400 Killed in Two Years

Known unionists were killed either by hired gunmen or by the so-called "Free unions" including Pau Sabater (1919), Evelino Boal (1921) and Salvador Seguí (1923), among other names that

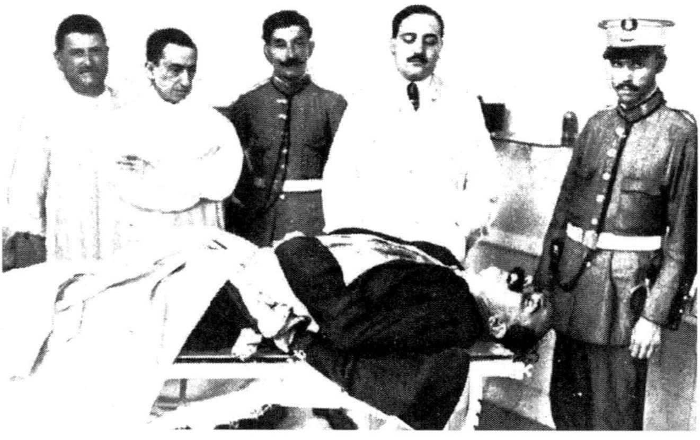

The body of Manuel Bravo Portillo, killed by the CNT in 1919.

have been lost in the course of those years of social warfare. Also, extremist and terrorist groups from the CNT for example, the *Los Solidarios* group, created in 1922 claimed their victims and assassinated Bravo Portillo (1919), the Count of Salvatierra (1920), and Dato (1921). In 1919, there were 109 social attacks in Barcelona. The following year, it would triple.

An Eye for an Eye, A Death for a Death

The personality of Manuel Bravo Portillo (? – 1919) remains hazy because while he "collaborated" with his country as a member of the police, he also worked as a spy for the German secret services.

Anti-communist propaganda from the Free Unions.

Assigned as the police commissioner in Barcelona since 1909, he assisted the Captain General of Catalonia, Joaquim Milans del Bosch, in repressing overly radical and noisy labour leaders. Initially, he employed hired gunmen, and later he took control of the Sindicatos Libres (Free Unions). Everything suggests that Bravo Portillo ordered the assassination of Barcelona businessman Josep Barret Moner on the orders of Baron de Rolland, who was in the service of the Germans. It is not entirely clear why Barret was targeted by the Kaiser's agents. Angel Pestaña criticized him in the *Solidaritat Obrera* Workers' Solidarity newspaper, and he could not refute the accusation and was imprisoned. Interestingly, the murder of one of the key witnesses for the prosecution allowed him to be released. He did not return to the police force but continued to dedicate his efforts to the Free Unions. As a reprisal for the murder of labour leader Pau Sabater, he died in September 1919 on Còrsega Street in Barcelona at the hands of radical anarcho-syndicalists.

The Dismemberment of Sales

With the proclamation of the Second Republic, Lluís Companys signed the Hunger Pact, in which employers agreed with the CNT and UGT that they would not hire any workers who belonged to the Free Unions.

Faced with this situation, its founder, Ramon Sales Amenós (1893-1936), went into exile in France. However, he returned to Barcelona in October 1936 to support the Francoist side. One day, he was recognised by former comrades of victims of the Free Unions while walking along the Rambla. The reaction was immediate: the workers rushed towards him and paralyzed him. Salas was then tied to four trucks that simultaneously started their engines and dismembered him.

Public Transport in Barcelona

A horse-drawn omnibus used to take the schoolchildren to Barceloneta, around 1875.

The exponential growth of the population in Barcelona forced the development of public transportation services. Before the widespread arrival of cars, these services were the only option for getting from one place to another. Barcelona had to make progress in this regard if it wanted to be on a par with major European cities.

The Major Technological Innovations

Music arrived in the home with the phonograph.

In addition to the installation of electrical supply in Barcelona, new inventions, born out of the industrial revolution, made life easier for the city's residents. In 1848, the first locomotives appeared, by 1877, the most basic telephones were already in operation, and a year later, the phonograph arrived. The city's growth created the need for new services. Until well into the 19th century, citizens with limited means would travel on foot, while the affluent would make use of horses or carriages. Horse-drawn vehicles, whether private or for hire, were the sole non-individual means of transportation employed in Barcelona. Nonetheless, the roads were neither easy to use nor accessible. Most of them were local routes, unsuitable for landaus in relatively comfortable conditions. The only passable roads were the international ones.

The Grandfather of Public Transportation

By the mid-19th century, the first horse-drawn coaches arrived, serving as collective means of transportation. Despite having a set route, there were no predetermined stops. Passengers themselves would signal where they wanted to get off, and those looking to get on would wait at some point along the route and signal the driver. The schedule followed certain patterns, but in a rather flexible manner, as the coach wouldn't commence its journey until it was full. This was the established methodology, and no one complained.

In 1852, the first horse-drawn tram was introduced in Paris, designed by Alphonse Loubat.

A Coal Mine Inspires the First Trains

The tramway was undoubtedly the most popular fixed-route public transportation of the 19th century. The coal mines small railcars, moving along tracks, served as the origin of the tramway in England. However, it was the French engineer Alphonse Loubat (1799-1866) who invented the requisite rail, made from iron and steel. Consequently, in 1852, the first horse-drawn tram was introduced in Paris. London followed suit in 1858, Geneva in 1862, and Madrid in 1869. Barcelona didn't overlook this invention, and in 1864, with the initiative of engineers Vila and Rafael de Luna, a project for a "double tram" was presented. It would run from Drassanes to Gràcia. This vehicle had room for only a few passengers, with an upper deck referred to as the "imperial" and was pulled by horses. It had to cover a distance of 7,000 metres between Pla de la Boqueria and Josepets. The tram was inaugurated on June 26, 1872, on Passeig de Gràcia, at four o'clock in the afternoon, amidst a grand celebration.

The first horse-drawn trams in Barcelona. Below, the spectacular and cumbersome steam tram crossing the city streets.

Steam Transforms Transport

In 1877, another significant achievement occurred when the first steam trams were introduced. These were remarkable vehicles consisting of a locomotive and three carriages, one for first-class and two for second-class passengers. To the astonishment of the citizens, these new inventions appeared at a dizzying speed for the era. Imagine, then, the excitement generated by the electric tram that started operating in 1895.

A Blue Tram, Almost Like a Toy

In 1898, the pharmacist and philanthropist Salvador Andreu established the Tibidabo joint-stock company. The company was intended to serve as a means urbanise the mountain on its slope closest to the city and to make access to the summit quick and easy, the idea of connecting the mountain with a tram and a funicular was conceived.

This was the summit of Tibidabo in 1901 when the first funicular started arriving. On the right, the famous *Tramvia Blau* (Blue Tram), which is still preserved today as a relic for tourism.

In the year 1901, the construction of Tibidabo Avenue was completed, and Spain's first funicular was inaugurated. The railway consisted of two carriages with a capacity for eighty passengers and covered one thousand eight hundred meters in eight minutes. The starting point was the current Doctor Andreu Square, named in his honour. To reach the foot of the funicular, an electric tram was installed: it was the *Tramvia Blau*, which travelled twelve hundred meters along Tibidabo Avenue.

SOME INFO

Doctor Andreu created cough drops called *Pastillas del Doctor Andreu,* which are still available in pharmacies today.

Did you know?
In 1965, the trams ceased to operate along Passeig de Gràcia, the street where their inauguration had been celebrated with great joy.

Miquel Biada.

The First Peninsula Train Departs from Passeig de Gràcia

Miquel Biada (1789-1848) was a merchant from Mataró who had gone to seek his fortune in Venezuela and Cuba when they were Spanish colonies. Precisely in Cuba, in 1837, he participated in the construction of the first railway that was inaugurated on the island. Upon his return, he settled back in his hometown. Popular memory tells of the day when Biada tried to board the stagecoach that travelled the 30 kilometres between Mataró and Barcelona but couldn't find a seat. After that uncomfortable situation, the entrepreneur began to conceive the perfect route for a new means of transportation that would be introduced in the country. Biada succeeded in founding the Great Spanish Iron Road Company from Barcelona to Mataró and Vice Versa in 1844. This company aimed to build the first train in the peninsular territory. And so, it did, developing the only means of transportation at the time capable of accommodating four hundred passengers per trip.

With the Train Comes the Bogeyman

Not everyone dreamed of this invention. Legend has it that the large convoys instilled fear in people, who saw them as the work of the devil.

It was said that the wheels, axles, and other gears of the contraption needed grease to function properly. There was a rumour that the best grease came from small children. Parents would tell their children that a man, *el hombre del saco* (the bogeyman), roamed the streets at night to kidnap children, kill them, extract the grease from their bodies, and thus allow the accursed invention to continue functioning.

Biada was in charge of the company until his death, one month before the inauguration of the first train. He never recovered from the pneumonia he had contracted while monitoring the railroad works to prevent acts of vandalism. You see, during the construction of the train, many people would come to the works at night to destroy what had been done during the day. It was an innovative mode of transportation, and it was challenging to get it accepted as such.

Did you know?
On the 28th of October 1848, the first railway in Spain was officially inaugurated.

Following London's Lead, The Metro Arrives in Sarrià

The Sarrià train was the work of the Barcelona to Sarrià Railway Company. The railway line was inaugurated in 1863 with steam locomotives. It was the first urban railway in Spain and the second in the world, as the London Underground had started its services just six months earlier. Initially conceived as a suburban train, the absorption of Gràcia, Sarrià, and Sant Gervasi changed its nature and made it an urban railway. At the beginning of the 20th century, it was electrified, and in 1915, the promoters of *La Canadenca* created the *Ferrocarrils de Catalunya* company, which took over the Sarrià train and modernised it.

Very Wide Platforms

In the early 20th century, Barcelona's traffic chaos led to many accidents. The most severe one occurred in 1925 when a train coming from Les Planes derailed, resulting in twenty-six deaths and

The Sarrià station in the year 1865.

Locomotive from the old Sarrià railway, which later served the Vallès line.

eighty-seven injured. With such a background, burying the Sarrià train became an urgent necessity, and in 1929, coinciding with the International Exhibition, the underground section was ready for its debut.

On the eve of the inauguration, on April 24, 1929, the traffic supervisors were astonished to discover that the trains couldn't enter the stations because the platforms had become too wide. In a project of this scale, the builders had not coordinated with the machine operators. On the verge of a nervous breakdown, the responsible parties assembled extra teams of workers who laboured throughout the night to trim the platforms.

The War For Control Of Four Wheels

A *La Catalana* ripert with medicinal advertising, at the end of the 19th century.

The *La Catalana* company was the most significant ripert enterprise in Barcelona. Riperts were old collective carriages, without tracks, pulled by two or four mules. Seeing the impact caused by electrified trams and desiring to compete in urban transportation, the company's officials set their sights on a revolutionary novelty that had made its first appearance in Paris in 1905: double-decker vehicles with gasoline engines. The company requested permission from the city council to change their riperts pulled by horses for these buses. They would travel

The first bus service in Barcelona was inaugurated in 1906, consisting of five vehicles that operated the route from Catalunya Square to Trilla Square in Gràcia.

from Plaça Catalunya Catalonia Square to Trilla Square in Gràcia through La Rambla de Catalunya. Despite objections from tram companies, Barcelona managed to launch its bus service in August 1906.

The first bus line had five units, and the fare was five cents less than the tram. Before seven in the morning, the ticket was half price. Public transportation had proven to be an excellent source of profit because it was used by many people.

In response, the Spanish entrepreneur Mariano de Foronda, the second Marquess of Foronda (1873-1961) and director of the Electric Tram Company of Barcelona, launched a fierce boycott. The Marquess repeatedly filed complaints with the city council, claiming that the new vehicles were noisy, travelled at over eight kilometres per hour, and caused, according to him, many accidents. The truth was that the buses struggled uphill to Gràcia and had little power. These difficulties, combined with the pressure exerted by Foronda's influence, ultimately led to the downfall of the company. The *La Catalana* adventure came to an end in 1908.

The Second Round of Buses

The buses had been withdrawn, but by 1920, it became clear that the trams couldn't cope. With the intention of improving services, the council asked Foronda to provide more units. However, post-European war conditions wouldn't allow him to meet the demand. The city council seized the opportunity to open the door again for buses. New challenges, protests, and complaints from Foronda didn't take long to arise. But faced with an urgent need, the automotive entrepreneur Alfredo Arruga and lawyer and politician Lluís Puig de la Bellacasa (1886-1960) obtained permission to create the General Bus Company of Barcelona. In 1924, Foronda realized that he couldn't stop progress out of fear of competition and decided to join forces with the enemy. Thus, he began by purchasing some shares in the new company. In a few years, he gained control of the company and eliminated tram competition by making buses and trams complementary.

Double-decker vehicle of the General Bus Company of Barcelona.

Safety Tests for Your Peace of Mind

When the upper deck of some buses was covered in 1930, rumours started circulating in the streets that the vehicle could easily overturn. The company decided to prove these rumours false with a demonstration: one of the buses was placed on a platform that tilted up to thirty degrees.

Did you know?
The company had permission to carry out special services for bullfights, horse races, and football matches.

SOME INFO

The Marquis of Foronda was appointed as the director of the 1929 International Exhibition of Barcelona.

From the Subway Ride to The City's Underground

A Subway Ride

The Grott mine train, inaugurated in 1906, was Barcelona's first subway.

Barcelona's first subway was an almost toy-like specimen, complete with coloured light bulbs and garlands. Engineer Carles Emili Montañès, the driving force behind *La Canadenca* and *Ferrocarrils de Catalunya*, was aware of the existence of the Grott mine, a tunnel just under a kilometre in length that connected Barcelona to the Vallvidrera reservoir. It had been built to transport water from the lagoon to Sarrià, but the company that operated it had to close due to financial problems. So, Montañès devised a way to fit a small electric train into the corridor for people who wanted to go to the Collserola mountains in maximum comfort.

It opened in June 1908. With a capacity of thirty-two passengers, it made the journey in six minutes and had eighty coloured light bulbs placed along its route. The invention was so successful that Tibidabo Amusement Park and the Sarrià train did everything they could to close it. The Grott mine train closed to the general public in 1909, although it continued to operate for transport workers and materials for *Ferrocarrils de Catalunya* for a little while longer.

The Early Challenges of The Metro's Life

The establishment of the metro in Barcelona was sporadic and tumultuous, with labour disputes included. After the Great War, in 1920, a society called *Ferrocarril Metropolitano de Barcelona* was created with capital from Catalan, Basque, and French entrepreneurs. This company decided to implement a project that had already existed since 1906: connecting Sants with Sant Martí de Provençals. Two years later, considering the magnitude of the task and its importance to the city, the city council joined the project by purchasing such a large number of shares in the new company that ended up becoming a semi-public company.

Metro construction on Las Ramblas and beneath Via Laietana.

The following year, *Banco de Vizcaya, Hispano Colonial,* and some Catalan entrepreneurs including *Ferrocarrils de Catalunya* and the Marquess of Foronda established the company *Gran Metropolitano de Barcelona,* which would be responsible for connecting Ciutadella with Bonanova. After many years of economic and bureaucratic waiting, there would not be just one metro but two.

Hesitations, Strikes, Water, and Finally, the Grand Metro

The initial plan would transform time and time again, with changes in destinations and possible station locations included. When construction works finally started, the impact of the social protests became evident. You see, the general strike declared after the assassination of Noi del Sucre on the 23rd of March 1923 had a direct impact on the building of the metro.

In December 1924, the Catalunya-Lesseps stretch was inaugurated, with subsequent extensions. However, the setbacks didn't stop there. The tunnels of Via Laietana were narrow, and when they attempted to widen them, significant water leaks appeared. It became necessary to install pumps to remove millions of litres of water each month. Due to technical issues, this second line wasn't completed until 1934.

In the forties, new trains were purchased. But these brand-new machines soon started experiencing minor malfunctions and inexplicable failures. The employees dubbed these irregularities as *jaimitadas* (pranks/japes). Almost automatically, the vehicles came to be known as *Jaimitos*.

The Metro Cars' Overheating

In the initial days of the metro's operation, it was discovered that the machine bearings overheated. After giving up on all the standard lubricants due to their lack of effectiveness, Engineer Francesc Planell decided to try his luck with castor oil. And it worked.

Pharmacies and drugstores in Sants were surprised by the sudden massive purchase of laxatives by the metro workers. The news of this curious behaviour inevitably spread throughout the neighbourhood, and that's how the rumour started that travelling on the metro caused intestinal problems. People had been talking about the metro construction for a while, and when the lines were inaugurated, the population turned out in large numbers to observe how an underground train worked. Despite the initial curiosity shown, people didn't take to using the service as often as anticipated. To help citizens overcome

Working conditions underground during that time weren't particularly healthy.

The residents of Barcelona didn't use the service as frequently as expected. In this 1942 picture, a tube train arrives at Sarrià station.

their fears, it is said that company employees made a habit of greeting each passenger as they boarded the trains. Despite their efforts, none of the lines met expectations until some years later.

The History of Taxis

In line with the buses, the first petrol-powered taxis appeared in Barcelona in 1906. Initially, there was only one rank on Las Ramblas, which had six cars. These taxis coexisted with horse-drawn rental carriages until the end of World War I.

In the history of taxis, there are some significant milestones, such as the introduction of car registration imposed by the *Guardia Urbana* city police force in 1907. By 1924, there were already sixty taxi ranks, and the city council established the Traffic Code, specifying that taxis should bear a coloured stripe across their doors to distinguish them from private cars. Over time, the yellow stripe became the standard.

The need for transportation during the Spanish Civil War led to the confiscation of taxis. This, coupled with a shortage of fuel and spare parts, eventually led to the suspension of the service. In 1939, the business would be reinstated, but only for the purpose of transporting authorities. The limited number of automobiles and the shortage of fuel forced the reuse of horse-drawn carriages.

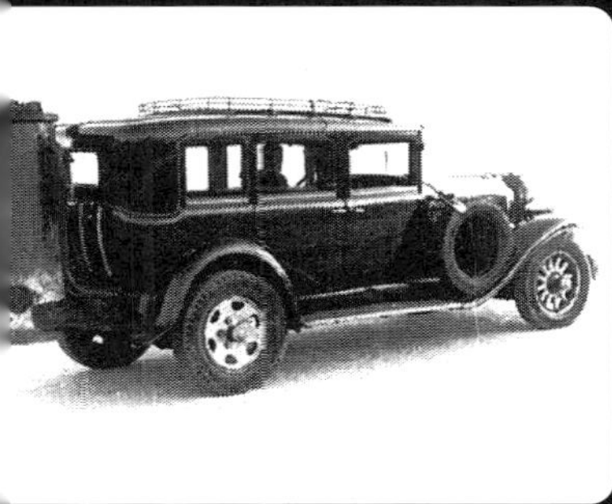

From top to bottom, different models of taxis in Barcelona: 1910, 1924, 1939, 1958, and 1985.

The revival of the taxi industry resumed when the Spanish Society of Touring Cars SEAT renewed the fleet in 1955. Since the distribution of licenses had been done with unclear criteria, their activity began to be regulated by the Metropolitan Corporation, which ceased to exist in 1988 and was replaced by the Metropolitan Transport Entity to coordinate all communication and transportation services. The number of taxis would continue to grow over the years, eventually turning these vehicles into undeniable icons of the streets of Barcelona.

4. Art, Culture, And Entertainment In A City That's Always In Fashion

The Literature of Barcelona

Could You Please Give Me a Love Letter?

In the past, the profession of scribes was considered to have divine origin because they were the ones who transmitted the word of the gods and gave it a permanent character. But there were scribes not only for the word of God, as there were also copyists and calligraphers who earned their living in the markets where, with their quills, inks, and papyrus, they wrote what the people on the street dictated to them: wills, pleas, and love letters. Illiteracy was endemic until very recently. That's why, at the beginning of the 20th century, it was still common to find scribes along the Rambles of Barcelona.

About Vocabulary
Before the appearance of the ballpoint pen, those who wanted to write had to do so with the help of bird feathers. Since their tips often wore out, they had to constantly trim them with a small knife, called a penknife.

The Most Political Poetry

It was the time of Joan I the Hunter (1350-1396) when Catalan was consolidating, and Romanesque architecture was giving way to Gothic. In addition to aesthetic changes, the thinking of the time was also experiencing new days: Humanism was taking shape, which would place the human being at the centre of the world. From a cultural perspective, the classical Greek and Latin authors were back in fashion. Influenced by these changes, the strongmen of Juan I saw the need to promote the Catalan language to prevent Italian and Castilian cultural policies from absorbing it. The writer and politician Lluís d'Avençó (1350? -1412/1415),

1490 engraving depicting a troubadour condemned to the gallows.

Did you know?
Martí the Humane was one of the most prestigious and powerful monarchs in the Christian world.

author of a dictionary of rhymes entitled *Torcimany*, persuaded the Count of Barcelona to hold an annual public event, mimicking one that was already taking place in Toulouse. It would provide Catalan poets with the opportunity to publicly recite their best work. On the 20th of February 1393, the Count issued a decree authorizing a poetry contest to be held every year during the week of the Assumption or the following one. And so, the Floral Games were born.

Joan I soon realized that such an event would be costly and entrusted his secretary, Bernat Metge, with seeking financial support from the *Consell de Cent*. Metge wrote a heartfelt letter to this institution, requesting the support of the councillors for such a noble purpose. However, the one hundred councillors, doubting that political solutions were found in the *Gaya Ciencia*, decided to ignore the request. We would have to wait for the decision of Martí the Humane, who assumed that the prize for the contest would come from the royal treasury, to see how the Floral Games eventually became a prestigious competition.

SOME INFO

Torcimany is considered one of the most important Catalan grammars of the medieval era.

Dark Dealings of the King's Right-Hand Man

Bernat Metge of Barcelona (1340/46-1413), the foremost representative of Catalan Humanism, was the central figure in one of the most notorious scandals of the

Lo somni, the masterpiece of Bernat Metge.

time. He served as secretary to Joan I, in addition to being a writer and translator of works by personalities such as Bocaccio. But besides literature, the man had another great passion: the market. He lived passionately with the bustling ant hill of people that gathered there: merchants, sailors, traders etc. For Metge, the market was the reflection of what Barcelona had to become someday: culturally strong, but also on a commercial and financial level.

Edition of *Lo somni* The Dream (1891).

Fate had it that an Italian merchant named Luqui Scarampo crossed paths with Metge and got him involved in rather shady business. They were so shady that the king's secretary ended up in prison accused of collecting undue commissions. He spent five years in jail, where he wrote *Lo somni* (The Dream), a key work in Catalan literature. Metge, amidst dreams and spectres, speaks of the uncertain moments he had to live through, of a time that will come, of a different future for the city and for its people. He exalts the figure of the king with abundant symbolism, in a dream of hope for his city that needs to become a nation. Upon his release from prison, Metge returned to work as a secretary in the Royal Chancellery until the death of Joan I in 1410.

Barcelona, the setting for Don Quixote's final battle

It is known that Miguel de Cervantes (1547-1616) spent a few months in Barcelona between the publication of the first and second parts of his most famous work. The writer's fascination with the city is expressed through the words of Don Quixote's protagonists. The sea, the port, the people, the friends among the locals, everything displays a Barcelona that seems extraordinary to the amazed eyes of the last knight of all times and his resigned companion.

After a brief maritime adventure with a wide-eyed Sancho Panza, Don Quixote heads to the Comellas printing press. In that scene, the writer creates a delirious situation: in this business,

EL INGENIOSO
HIDALGO DON QVI-
XOTE DE LA MANCHA,
Compuesto por Miguel de Ceruantes
Saauedra.
DIRIGIDO AL DVQVE DE BEIAR,
Marques de Gibraleon, Conde de Benalcaçar, y Bañares, Vizconde de la Puebla de Alcozer, Señor de
las villas de Capilla, Curiel, y
Burguillos.
Año, 1605.
CON PRIVILEGIO,
EN MADRID, Por Iuan de la Cuesta.
Vendese en casa de Francisco de Robles, librero del Rey nro señor.

Engraving by Gustave Doré depicting Don Quixote on his way to his final duel, on the beach of Barcelona. To the right, the first edition, from 1605.

they print none other than the false Quixote by Alfonso Fernández de Avellaneda. Cervantes takes advantage of the pages of the second part of his novel to expose the appearance of the fraudulent Quixotic volume.

Don Quixote will live on the beach of Barcelona his final duel, the last one: if he loses, he'll have to return home and leave behind his out-of-context knightly adventures. And, facing the Knight of the White Moon, he is defeated. Defeated, Quixote sets out on the journey back home, where he will abandon his delusions forever.

SOME INFO

Although there is no document to corroborate it, they say that when Cervantes visited Barcelona, he stayed at number 2, Paseo de Colom. The house can still be seen just as it was in the 16th century.

The Invisible Years of Catalan

The historical events of the 18th century had disastrous consequences for Catalan culture and language. Universities disappeared, and the only existing centre of higher education, the University of Cervera, remained attached to Latin and despised Humanism. The bourgeoisie showed no cultural interests, and the aristocracy became Hispanized. Writers in cultured Catalan language disappeared because they saw Catalan as an outdated and backward cultural tool. Only a few intellectuals would remain faithful to their mother tongue, defending it from foreign influences.

Although Catalan will disappear as an official language with the New Plant Decree, its use will continue among the common people. It will continue to be used in popular genres, which no one hinders because they are considered minor. In families, among friends, and in the squares, a Catalan popular narrative will be maintained with stories, legends, poetry, and proverbs. Religious and secular popular theatre will also continue to be performed in Catalan.

During these years, there will be a great dialectal segmentation of the language since for a period of two hundred years, official usage norms cannot be established.

Above, the University of Cervera. Below, the statue of Bonaventura Carles Aribau, the author of *Oda a la Pàtria* (Ode to the Homeland).

The Literary Renaissance of a Language

The 19th century would not only be industrially prosperous but would also mark the resurgence of cultured Catalan language. Catalan resumed its trajectory as a literary language in 1833 when the Barcelona writer Bonaventura Carles Aribau (1798-1862) published *Oda a la Pàtria* (Ode to the Homeland). This phenomenon is not unrelated to the emergence of Romanticism in Europe, which arrived somewhat later in Catalonia, becoming the catalyst the country needed to reclaim its identity and radically transform Catalan culture in the 19th century. The cultural movement accompanying this change will be known as *La Renaixença* (The Renaissance).

Jacint Verdaguer, a Poet with Angels and Demons

When Jacint Verdaguer (1845-1902) published *Oda a Barcelona* (Ode to Barcelona), the impact it had was such that in the blink of an eye, he became "the poet of Barcelona". In an extraordinary move for the time, the city council produced a hundred thousand copies of the work.

Jacint Verdaguer, the great Catalan poet.

Always closely connected to the archdiocese of Vic, Verdaguer accepted a journey with the shipping company of Antonio López y López, Marquess of Comillas, as an inspector of the company's priests. His maritime adventure, lasting about two years, surely influenced him when writing *L'Atlàntida* (Atlantis). Upon his return from the journey, he became a private priest for the Comillas family and had a monastic cell on Canuda Street.

Now a hugely popular writer, Verdaguer couldn't accept the idea that the Marquess of Comillas was involved in the trafficking of African slaves. Motivated by this fact, he decided to distribute the businessman's money among those in need, and in response to this action, the Marquess severed ties with the clergyman.

Sculptural ensemble in Jacint Verdaguer Square in Barcelona.

Father Joaquim Pinyol introduced Verdaguer to the practice of exorcisms, which contributed to the rejection by many. Only a few friends understood the poet's crisis and stood by him until the end. Considering the rumours, the Bishop of Vic revoked Verdaguer's priestly license and sent him to the sanctuary of *La Gleva*, but the poet interpreted this gesture as an exile. During this time, his health began to weaken, and rumours spread that his mental state was altered. Fearing that he would be perceived as insane, Verdaguer retracted his actions before the bishop of Vic, who returned his license. However, the writer passed away due to tuberculosis in 1902 at Vil·la Joana, a property in Vallvidrera.

Did you know?
One of the most frequently repeated street names throughout Catalonia.

According to a biography of the writer Sebastià Juan Arbó (1902-1984), the flower sellers on Las Ramblas threw so many flowers as Verdaguer's funeral procession passed by that the poet walked away on a thick floral carpet. This popular tribute brought to life the verse: "jamay tanta florida s'és vista en son jardí" (never have so many blossoms been seen in his garden) from his Ode to Barcelona. His body was buried in Montjuïc cemetery.

Joan Maragall: The Poet of Tumultuous Barcelona

Joan Maragall (1860-1911) is the clearest exponent of social Romanticism in Barcelona's poetry. In his work, the city of Barcelona is the object of love, fear, and concern. Throughout his life, Maragall would constantly critique Catalan bourgeois society, balancing his romantic non-conformism with an awareness of the country's problems and reality.

Joan Maragall.

Maragall lived through turbulent times, and it hit close to home as he was present at the Liceu when an anarchist bombed it one night. Like everyone else, he did what he could, and like everyone else, he was left in shock. Upon returning home, watching his wife breastfeeding their small child, he would write a text entitled *Paternal*:

Fury is bursting forth with hatred for the land,
bloody heads are gifted by the harrowing shears,
and one must go to the festivities
with a determined chest, as in war.
With each deadly outburst - people tremble
and turn:
The cruelty that advances - the fear that
withdraws:
They are dividing the world...
Looking at the nursing child, - the sighing mother,
The father furrows his brow.

But the innocent child,
Who, satisfied, leaves the drained breast,
Looks at himself, - looks at herself, and laughs wildly.

The events of the *Setmana Trágica* (Tragic Week) also left a deep impression on him. Maragall published some articles in which he expressed his concern about what was happening and would leave a piece of work, *Oda nova a Barcelona* (New Ode to Barcelona), where he engaged in a dialogue with a city he loved, despite how difficult he found it to understand her.

The Man Who Introduced Cinema to Barcelona

Fructuós Gelabert in the year 1955.

It was the year 1896 when the Napoleón brothers, owners of the most prominent photography studio in Barcelona, organised a session in their workshop to see the Lumière cinematograph in action. While some of the attendees began to flee in terror, a young man obsessed with Edison's kinetoscope remained rooted to the spot. That boy had been fatally injured by what he had seen: his first film. He was Fructuós Gelabert (1874-1955) from Gràcia, who, although he was not a newcomer to the world of the image six years previously, he had contacted the

Napoleón family and had already built a camera, his initial encounter with moving images captivated him forever. Gelabert would be the pioneer of cinema in Spain alongside Segundo de Chomón.

With the photographer Santiago Biosca, whom he met a year after the inspiring film session, they successfully created a device similar to that of the Lumière brothers. Together, they filmed two documentaries: *Departure of Workers from La España Industrial Factory* and *Departure of the Congregation from the Parish Church of Santa María de Sants.* Eager to go a step further, with the help of friends from the neighbourhood, he made *Riña en un café* (Brawl in a café), a short film inspired by the Lumière brothers' *The Sprinkler Sprinkled. Riña en un café* would be the first Spanish film with a storyline. It was so successful that Gelabert decided to open a cinema, but the business did not prosper as he had hoped.

Two versions of the first Catalan film, *Brawl in a Café* (1897).

A Pioneer in Everything

Gelabert was a pioneer in the world of moving images. He was the first to conceive of cinema as an industry, creating the country's first film studios. He was also the first to make a cinematic transaction from the Iberian Peninsula to abroad with the film *Visita de doña Cristina y don Alfonso XIII a Barcelona* (The visit of lady Cristina and Alfonso XIII to Barcelona), a documentary about the visit of the royals to the city. Furthermore, he was the first to experiment with cinematic special effects in the movie *Choque de dos transatlánticos* (Collision of two ocean liners), where he used miniature ships.

Gelabert was an extraordinary inventor and a true pioneer in the language of cinema. But the First World War and the Spanish Civil War would halt their brilliant future, and the creator would die in 1955 in poverty and obscurity. The meagre material that remains of his work is stored in a warehouse at the *Museu de la Ciència i la Tècnica de Catalunya* in Terrassa.

SOME INFO

When the films *Guardia burlada* and *Los calzoncillos de Toni* (Toni's briefs), both from 1908, were projected, the actors from the Teatro Romea read the dialogues of the story hidden behind the scenes, creating a sensation of sound cinema.

Did you know?
After filming the comedy *Los guapos de la vaquería del parque* (The boys from the park dairy) Gelabert received an offer to work in the United States, but he turned it down.

Àngel Guimerà: From Theatre To Cinema

Àngel Guimerà (1845-1924), the leading figure of the *Renaixença* theatre, was fortunate to see two pieces of his work adapted into films. Fructuós Gelabert turned *Terra baixa* (Lowland) and *Maria Rosa* into movies. They say that the playwright was deeply moved when he watched his works projected on a screen.

Narcís Oller: Reality Engages in the Novel

Bust of Narcís Oller, created by Eusebi Arnau.

Industrialisation is closely tied to the emergence of the working class and its issues. Considering that during the 19th century, Barcelona was one of the most industrialised cities in Europe, it seems natural that the first literary currents of social content began to emerge there: realism and naturalism.

The foremost representative of Catalan realism is Narcís Oller (1846-1930). The author's preferred themes were industrialisation, the tensions between the countryside and the city, and the individual's struggle to adapt to the new reality. Among his other significant work, he wrote *La Papallona* (The Butterfly), *L'escanyapobres* (The Leech), and *La febre d'or* (Gold Fever). In the latter, Oller meticulously portrays the industrial Barcelona of the 19th century.

Architectural Modernism

Many Catalan industrial bourgeois families chose to invest a portion of their income in the construction of true architectural monuments.

Memories of Casa Lleó Morera at the Dalí Museum

Casa Lleó Morera originated from the renovation of an existing building. The project, designed by Lluís Domènech i Montaner, took two years to materialise (1904-1906). The defining characteristic of this building was its Wagnerian atmosphere, very vogue among the bourgeoisie of Barcelona at the time. The facade is crowned by an elegant temple

Casa Lleó Morera, designed by Lluís Domènech i Montaner, on Passeig de Gràcia.

with eight columns. Originally, the facade was covered with columns and statues, but when they wanted to install a shop on the ground floor, they were removed, and many believed that all had been destroyed. In reality, though, the house porter managed to save some pieces. Upon learning this, Salvador Dalí bought the statues he liked the most for very little money. Now, one of them can be seen at the Dalí Museum in Figueres.

Did you know?
In 1906, this house received the first architecture award granted by the city council.

SOME INFO

The name of the house doesn't correspond to the surname of its owners, but rather refers to the decorative symbols inspired by medieval shields that Domènech i Montaner placed on the façade.

The Palau Güell, a Building that Came Close to Going to The Americas

The first significant commission that Gaudí received was the project for the Palau Güell. Eusebi Güell i Bacigalupi, Count Güell and son-in-law of the Marquess of Comillas, a friend and follower of the architect from Reus, entrusted him with this residence.

Although the decoration work continued until 1890, the house was inaugurated in 1888, coinciding with the celebration of the Universal Exhibition of Barcelona.

The architect created a spectacular entrance with arched doors and wrought iron gates. To accommodate carriages, the entrance

Two images of Palau Güell, designed by Gaudí.

was of considerable dimensions. Inside, the wooden and iron ceilings in the Mudéjar style stand out. As is customary in Gaudí's work, he designed several decorated chimneys on the roof. The basement space was left for the stables, which were accessed through a spiral ramp.

Eusebi Güell lived in the palace until 1906 when he moved to Casa Larrard in Park Güell, where he passed away in 1918. His family continued to reside in the building until the outbreak of the Civil War when the property was seized for use as a police station. Surprisingly, in 1944, an American millionaire wanted to buy the palace and transport it, piece by piece, to the United States. To save it from such disfigurement and prevent the cultural plundering of the city, the Barcelona Provincial Council stepped in and acquired it in advance.

Did you know?

This building, declared a UNESCO World Heritage Site in 1984, has been partially open to the public since 2008, when the Barcelona Provincial Council reopened it.

La Casa Amatller (The Amatller House): a Chocolate Building

In 1898, the chocolate industrialist Antoni Amatller purchased a building on Passeig de Gràcia to renovate it to his liking. He commissioned the work to the architect Josep Puig i Cadafalch, who completely renovated the facade, the lobby, the main floor, and the attic. The architect opted for an urban Gothic style with a facade that has Nordic influences, reminiscent of a chocolate bar. The main floor has been preserved just as it was originally. Sculptures are distributed throughout various spaces, seamlessly integrated into the ambiance conceived by the architect. Roman mosaics and white marble tiles cover the floors, and the ceilings are sgraffito decorated by cutting away parts of a surface layer to expose a different-coloured ground and supported by polychrome beams.

Josep Puig i Cadafalch's Amatller House is adorned with numerous small sculptures, such as this one of Saint George and the dragon.

Within the building, you'll find the Amatller Institute of Hispanic Art, established in 1941 by the industrialist's daughter, Teresa Amatller. It boasts a large library, a photographic archive, and a sound archive available to researchers and art historians.

On the pavement, there is a red stone marking the starting point of Catalan modernism, kilometre zero. This marker is located in front of all the modernist buildings on Passeig de Gràcia.

Park Güell: A House for Hansel and Gretel

In 1899, Eusebi Güell acquired two adjacent estates on Turó del Carmel, which was known as Bald Mountain at that time. He intended to build a development away from the city. The entrepreneur wanted to create high-quality spaces and buildings with a distinctive aesthetic that would blend seamlessly into the landscape. The initial project envisioned sixty houses scattered throughout the park, all surrounded by trees and gardens and with a privileged view of Barcelona. It was meant to be a development in an isolated, tranquil space, with all the benefits of being in contact with nature.

Güell and Gaudí collaborated on the conception of the park, which was built between 1900 and 1914. The two structures on either side of the main gate were inspired by the tale of Hansel and Gretel. When the architect began envisioning the project, the story of the two siblings was being performed as an opera at the Liceu. The house on the left is identified as the home of the two children, while the one on the right, with a poisonous mushroom on top, represents the witch's house.

Panoramic view of Barcelona from Park Güell.

Gaudí infused the entire park's design with the symbolism of three basic elements: nature, religion and Catalan identity. Thus, the space is laid out between rows of columns that resemble palm trees, stalactites, lava rivers, caves, and geometric shapes where the straight line is non-existent. The architect also had Mediterranean species planted so they would adapt perfectly to the terrain. And, taking advantage of the slope of the hillside, Gaudí constructed a pathway that on the original plans led to a church that was never built. In its place stands the Calvary monument, known as the Hill of Three Crosses.

Dual Purpose

The hypostyle hall, or the hall of a hundred columns, actually has only eighty-six. All the columns are hollow inside because they were designed to drain the water that flowed from the large oval square that crowns the hall. This water was supposed to flow into an underground reservoir of twelve thousand cubic metres, which, when filled, would release water from the mouth of the dragon located in the centre of the entrance staircase. This hall had been conceived as the market of the development.

The famous mosaic dragon of Park Güell.

The seats in the oval square were designed so that the human body could rest comfortably. Over several decades, Gaudí anticipated the current concept of ergonomics, the study of the shape and position of objects, furniture, or tools, adapting them to the anatomy of the human body.

One of the viaducts that crosses the park is named the Rosary because it is bordered by stone balls, like the beads of a rosary. It departs from the central square and crosses the park in a transverse direction. This viaduct was built on the remains of an ancient Roman road that led to Sant Cugat del Vallès.

About Vocabulary
The justification for the name in English, Park Güell, is found in the inspiration that Güell himself drew from Ebenezer Howard's Garden cities (1850-1928).

The Failure of an Idea Ahead of Its Time

Unfortunately, this extraordinary project was an economic failure. During those times, the bourgeoisie had not only embraced the criticised Eixample but also boasted of having palaces and houses in this place that expressed their social status and economic exuberance.

The first residence that was built was Count Güell's, Casa Larrard, to which its owner moved before the development of the urbanisation. Apart from this, only two more plots were sold. One was acquired by Gaudí himself, on which Francesc Berenguer, his favourite disciple, would build the home where the architect lived between 1906 and 1925. Martí Trias i Domènech, a friend of the two creators of the park, acquired the other plot, where Juli Batllevel built the third and final house in the urbanization. Although in 1906 the project showed no signs of success, construction continued until 1914 when it was suspended due to the start of the First World War. Güell died in 1918, and his heirs sold the park to the city council, which opened it as a public space in 1922.

SOME INFO

During the construction of the park, prehistoric caves were discovered.

Did you know?
In 1969, Park Güell was declared a National Historic-Artistic Monument, while in 1984, UNESCO designated it as a World Heritage Site.

Casa Batlló: A Home with No Room for the Piano

Josep Batlló i Casanovas owned a building at 43 Passeig de Gràcia, constructed by Emili Sala Cortés in 1877. However, in 1901, the owner applied for permission to demolish the existing building to erect a new one. Upon receiving a rejection, three years later, he made another attempt by applying to renovate the building. The project that Gaudí prepared for presentation to the authorities lacked detail. Surely, the architect wanted to avoid providing excessive information to prevent the discovery that he was not adhering to all the established construction regulations. Despite the ambiguity, the city council eventually granted the building permit.

The project involved transforming the facade and reorganising all the spaces within the house, creating more ventilated and illuminated environments. Two floors were added: one for the attic, adapted for the residence of the service staff, and the rooftop. Work commenced in 1904 and would be completed in two years. The facade is probably one of the most original and spectacular in the world. The central part, clad in polychrome ceramic, suggests a space of water with aquatic plants that ripple and come

Casa Batlló, on Passeig de Gràcia, "a glimpse of paradise."

to life with the reflection of coloured glass shards embedded in them. The highest part of the building is crowned by an rippling form covered with ceramic tiles, placed in such a way that they resemble the scales of a dragon. On the terrace, there are helical chimneys and a tower with a four-armed cross, which was to Gaudí's liking. The courtyard is adorned with white tiles at the bottom and blue tiles at the top, a clever idea to make better use of sunlight. The interior, entirely designed by Gaudí, features staircases, furniture, fireplaces, wooden windows, decorated glasswork, and other elements that reinforce the concept of originality.

The interior of Casa Batlló was entirely designed by Antoni Gaudí.

It is said that while Gaudí was building the interior of the building, Mrs. Batlló expressed her concern when she realized that there wouldn't be enough space for her daughter's grand piano. After the construction was completed, it was indeed evident that there was not enough room for the child's piano. Faced with this unavoidable fact, the artist advised the lady that her daughter should switch to playing the violin.

About Vocabulary
The building is popularly known as the "House of Bones." This name comes from the fact that on the first floor, the columns of the balcony have a bony appearance, and the balcony railings on the other floors may resemble skulls.

SOME INFO

Gaudí was asked, "What do you want to do with Casa Batlló?" The architect replied that he wanted to create "a vision of paradise."

Did you know?
The Batlló family sold the building in 1954 to the Iberia Insurance Society. In 1994, the house passed to the Bernat family. In 2005, it was recognized by UNESCO as a World Heritage Site.

The so-called Block of Discord is of unparalleled beauty.

A Block of Discord

The popularly called *Manzana de la Discordia* (Block of Discord) is situated to the left of Passeig de Gràcia, between Consell de Cent and Aragó streets. The houses of discord are Lleó Morera, Amatller, and Batlló. Their disagreement is not among themselves but among the countless opinions that accompanied their construction, with an extravagance completely foreign to the tastes of the nineteenth century. All three have some common features: they were all reconstructions and renovations of previously built houses, and, most importantly, the architects who created them, like all modernists, had the support of numerous skilled artisans who worked on the mosaics, ironwork, ceramics, stained glass, and decorative elements of the interiors.

The Pedrera: An Insult to the Bourgeois Class

Rumour has it that Casa Milà, despite being an initiative of Pere Milà i Camps, should have been called Casa Guardiola. Why, you ask? Some claim it was the fortune of Milà's wife's first husband, Josep Guardiola i Grau, that funded the construction.

A Wealthy and Seasoned Indiano

Josep Guardiola i Grau was born in L'Aleixar, a village near Reus, in 1831. He travelled to Guatemala as a young man and engaged in coffee cultivation. From one plantation to several, he eventually amassed a considerable fortune. After selling his properties, the merchant returned to Reus. Back home, he made various investments, but the most unexpectedly profitable one was in the *Compagnie Universelle du Canal Océanique,* tasked with constructing the Panama Canal designed by Ferdinand de Lesseps. Eventually, this company ran out of funds for the project, and Guardiola grew even richer when he sold the concession for the works to the United States. At the age of sixty, he married a young woman from Reus named Roser Segimon. Guardiola passed away shortly after the wedding, leaving behind a young and very wealthy widow.

Ten years later, Roser travelled to France. In Vichy, a fashionable spa town, she met Pere Milà, a young man from Barcelona from a very good family. Roser, captivated by the young man, married him. In 1905 at the behest of her husband, the Milàs purchased the house of Ferrer Vidal between Passeig de Gràcia and Provença Street. After lengthy discussions, Pere persuaded his wife to construct a building designed by Gaudí, who was at that time working on the Casa Batlló. The architect's aesthetics did not convince the widow, who did not find them suitable for her tastes or social status. Therefore, Milà implored the architect not to stray too far from the prevailing customs of the bourgeoisie and to avoid those "demonic" forms, an expression his wife had used to describe the already established style of that revolutionary of forms.

Gaudí presented a project to the couple in 1906. He added a figure of the Virgin to help smooth out any disagreements with the owner. The construction took four years, and during this time, there were several disputes with the city council, such as the case of a column that occupied part of the pavement and which the public corporation had removed. The city council also ordered the removal of the attic rooms because they exceeded the building's legal height by four metres. In this case, however, Gaudí's stubbornness and indifference to established rules managed to successfully overcome the ordeal. Casa Milà was completed in 1910 without the image of the Virgin. The Tragic Week of 1909 had been a decisive factor in the Milàs giving up on placing it.

The impressive *patio de luces* (lightwell).

When the building was completed, the prominent property owners in the area stopped greeting the Milàs. They believed that this property, so far removed from the neoclassical taste of the bourgeoisie, would lower the price of the surrounding houses, as no one would want to live near such an eccentric building. Disparagingly, they began to refer to the house as *La Pedrera* (The Quarry). Over the years, this name would stick, and today it is no longer considered a pejorative name.

Pere Milà died before his wife, who never fully embraced the aesthetics of the building. The woman completely remodelled it, but only after Gaudí's death. Despite their differences, Mrs. Milà always had great respect for the modernist architect.

SOME INFO

La Pedrera was the last civil building built by Gaudí.

Did you know?
UNESCO recognized it as a World Heritage monument in 1984.

Casa Fuster: The Most Expensive Building in Barcelona

Mariano Fuster i Fuster, a gentleman from Mallorcan high society, wanted to gift a house to his wife in the city where they had met. This is how he commissioned Lluís Domènech i Montaner to build a building at the end of Passeig de Gràcia, at number 132, opposite the Salvador Espriu Gardens.

At the time of its inauguration in 1911, it was considered the most expensive house in Barcelona due to the high quality of the materials used. In what would be Montaner's posthumous work in Barcelona, the architect collaborated with his son, Pere Domènech i Roura.

About Vocabulary
The gardens in front are known as Salvador Espriu Gardens because in one of the rooms of the cylindrical corner tower, the poet from Santa Coloma de Farners wrote part of his work.

Casa Fuster, at the beginning of Passeig de Gràcia, the majestic and posthumous work of Domènech i Montaner.

Did you know?
A hotel chain purchased the property a few years ago, completely transforming the interior and restoring the facade.

For many years, the building housed the Café Vienés, a place of gathering of the Catalan bourgeoisie. The building was on the brink of demolition in 1960 when the company ENHER bought it for eleven million pesetas, although a multitude of critical voices prevented its destruction.

The Sagrada Familia: Gaudí's Great Ambition

The bookseller and philanthropist Josep Maria Bocabella (1815-1892), founder of the Association of Devotees of Saint Joseph, wanted to create a temple dedicated to the Sagrada Familia (Holy Family). To this end, he acquired land between what are now the streets of Provença, Mallorca, Marina, and Sardenya. It was an uninhabited area, and the church would have ample space to be observed from a distance.

The beginnings of the Sagrada Familia, in the year 1915.

Josep Maria Bocabella.

Initially, the project was entrusted to the diocesan architect Francisco de Paula del Villar (1828-1901), who, after a year of work, resigned due to continuing disagreements with Joan Martorell, Bocabella's consultant architect. Faced with this setback, the bookseller offered Martorell himself the continuation of the project, but he suggested passing the commission to Antoni Gaudí, who at that time was his assistant. At the end of the year 1883, the man from Reus was thirty-one years old and, unknowingly, was about to begin his *magnum opus*. From then on, and for the next forty-three years, the last fifteen exclusively, Gaudí would dedicate himself to the construction of the temple.

The first stone was laid on March 19, 1882, Saint Joseph's Day, and the works began on August 25, 1883. With the commission in his hands, Gaudí changed Villar's project, except for the crypt, which had already been built, and he only modified the capitals.

The Sagrada Família is the prime example of Gaudí's architectural concept. It eliminates the straight line, typical of Gothic, which Gaudí found cold and disconnected from nature, and adopts the curve in all its expressions. The inclined columns eliminate the need for flying buttresses on the exterior and shift the forces towards the interior of the space, as occurs with the structures that the architect had observed in nature.

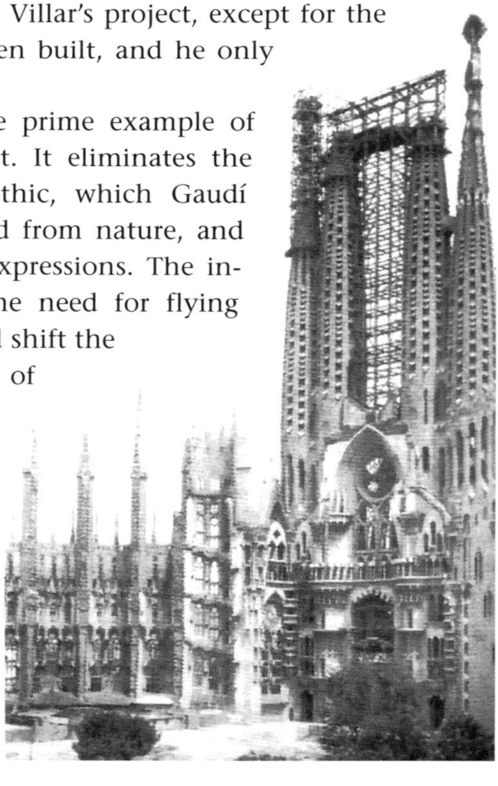

The temple's construction in 1928, as seen by Gaudí shortly before his death.

A Temple with Many Details

- The holy water fonts in the crypt are made with enormous seashells from the Felipepines.

- The porticos on the Nativity facade are separated by two huge columns, each resting on a turtle. The one facing Tibidabo is a land turtle, and the one facing the sea is a marine specimen.
- Gaudí only saw one tower completed, which served as a model for the construction of the others.

- The architect was buried in the crypt of the Temple, just like Josep Bocabella, but the latter's tomb was desecrated.
- On the Portico of Hope, you can see various scenes from the life of the child Jesus, including some representations of Joseph. When Gaudí died, the workers sculpted his face on the figure of Joseph as a tribute to the great architect.

- Gaudí had conceived the Nativity facade as a model to guide the continuation of the project after his death.
- Many of Gaudí's original documents, plans, and drawings were destroyed in a fire caused during the Civil War.

Throughout its history, the construction of the Sagrada Familia has experienced several interruptions, both due to economic problems and political reasons. It is believed that if the current work pace is maintained, the temple could be completed in the first third of this century.

About Vocabulary
The temple has always had the status of expiatory, meaning it has been and continues to be constructed solely with donations.

Antoni Gaudí, with a white beard, showcases the works of the Sagrada Família to the Vatican's nuncio, Francesco Ragonesi. On that occasion, Monsignor Ragonesi referred to Gaudí as «the Dante of architecture".

Did you know?
In 2005, the Nativity facade and the crypt were declared UNESCO World Cultural Heritage sites.

Antoni Gaudí: The Life of a Genius

Born in Reus, Antoni Gaudí (1852-1926) came from a family of coppersmiths. Although he leaned towards utopian socialist ideas during his youth, he later developed a avid passion for Catholicism. When conferring the title upon Gaudí, the director of the Barcelona School of Architecture, Elies Rogent, said, "We have granted a title to either a madman or a genius; time will tell". He never married and lived with his father and niece until their deaths. In 1906, he began residing in his property at Park Güell. The building had been constructed as a showhouse for the urbanisation and currently houses the Gaudí Museum.

Towards the end of his life, completely alone his family had died, as well as his close friends, he moved to live in a small room in the Sagrada Familia Temple. It was his habit to attend daily Mass at the church of Sant Felip Neri and he used to walk there. On one of his walks to the service, on June 7, 1926, while trying to cross Gran Via de les Corts Catalanes, between Bailén and Girona streets, Gaudí saw a tram approaching and stepped back to avoid it, but unfortunately, he was struck by the oncoming convoy.

Above, Gaudí's father and niece. To the left, the architect at the age of 32, and below, his burial in the temple's crypt in 1926.

Gaudí was badly injured, and none of the passing cars wanted to help him. He had not trimmed his beard in a long time, was wearing old clothes, and looked like a homeless man. The police took him to the Hospital de la Santa Creu, and he remained anonymous there until the priest from the Sagrada Familia, who was puzzled by his prolonged absence, found him. They wanted to transfer him to another hospital, but he refused because he said he felt comfortable among the poor. Before his death, he received visits from important figures in Barcelona, and the newspapers strongly criticised the pedestrians who had ignored the injured man. None of the car drivers in all of Barcelona admitted to being there. His funeral was attended by a large crowd.

About Vocabulary
Gaudí said: "The straight line belongs to men, the curve to God".

The Architect with the Greatest Number of Buildings in Barcelona

Enric Sagnier i Villavecchia (1858-1931) was the preferred architect of the bourgeois and Catholic classes of the time, and also the most prolific. There are around three hundred documented buildings by the architect throughout the city. He was the architect with the most projects carried out in Barcelona. In fact, it's almost impossible to walk down a street in the Eixample without encountering a Sagnier building.

With a more understated aesthetic compared to his contemporaries Domènech i Montaner, Puig i Cadafalch, and Gaudí, Sagnier's constructions were balanced and functional. Some of his most iconic buildings include *La Caixa de Pensions de Barcelona* on Vía Laietana, the Palace of Justice in the city, and the Expiatory Temple of the Sacred Heart on the top of Tibidabo. This would be his most prominent religious work, a monument that was completed by his eldest son, Josep Maria, after his father's death.

Enric Sagnier was the author of, among many buildings in Barcelona, the Expiatory Temple of the Sacred Heart of Tibidabo.

The Feather, Brush, and Musical Note Artists

The Most Famous Tertullian in Barcelona

Possibly for the first time, in the late 18th century, painters, writers, poets, musicians, and intellectuals began to gather in cafés to chat, exchange impressions, and discuss a bit of everything.

The *Lyon d'Or* was a café owned by Mr. Vilalta, a passionate collector of weapons and medieval objects that adorned the walls of his establishment. Journalists and writers like Carles Costa (1865-1926), Rafael Moragas (1883-1966), who was also a great cultural promoter of the time, and Màrius Verdaguer (1885-1963) used to attend this café. Verdaguer has left a firsthand account of this gathering, probably one of the most entertaining in Barcelona, as it had the presence of an incredibly imaginative conversationalist.

Pompeu Gener "Peius".

This was the polymath Pompeu Gener, Peius (1848-1920), who explained that his uncle had the idea of crossbreeding carrier pigeons with parrots because he wanted the offspring to be able to convey messages verbally. He also said that the same uncle had told him that an ancestor of the family, Genaro de Pimentel Prats de Gener, was besieged in the city of Utrecht. When they had exhausted all the projectiles, the man, quick-witted as he was, coated all the city's Edam cheeses in tar and used them as cannonballs, causing the enemies to flee in terror.

Peius had an imagination without limits. He could just as easily say that Baghdad had been such a vast city that it had a desert in its centre as claim to have met Sarah Bernhardt, the most important actress of the 19th century. He explained that the diva had invited him to her apartment and dressed as an odalisque chambermaid and flanked by two lions, had asked him to recite the *Cantar del Mío Cid* to improve her Spanish. People came

About Vocaulary
During the reign of Felipe IV (1605-1665), the writings and speeches of the writer Quintus Septimius Florens Tertullian (150/160? -220/240?), a great defender of Christianity who used surprising wordplay in his arguments, became fashionable. His speeches were so encouraging that they led to regular meetings where attendees spoke, debated, or praised the great orator. These meetings eventually became known as *tertulias*, and their attendees were called *tertulianos*.

to the gathering just to provoke Peius who, before any casually thrown word, could create a fantastic world of perpetual fabulation. In reality, he went to the gathering just to have fun.

The other side of Peius was that of a rigorous art critic. He was a man of science, he had studied Pharmacy and Natural Sciences, and he earned his doctorate from the University of Madrid. He also attended courses at the School of Fine Arts in Barcelona and published a book titled *La Mort et le Diable* (Death and the Devil, 1880) in French. He was a liberal, declaring himself against the monarchy, scholasticism, and neoclassicism because they were stiff and disconnected from reality. He was a positivist and deeply Darwinian. Peius had an eccentric personality. He was extreme both in the verbosity of the gathering and when discussing science. His funeral was attended by a huge crowd.

Els Quatre Gats: a Breeding Ground for Artists

Ramon Casas portrayed with style and irony the artists of the Els Quatre Gats gathering.

Pere Romeu (1862-1908), who had worked as an entertainer at the cabaret Le Chat Noir in Paris, wanted to open a place in Barcelona where the bohemian atmosphere he had seen in the French capital prevailed. Known to Ramon Casas (1866-1932) for his passion for painting, he was the soul of Els Quatre Gats (The Four Cats), the quintessential meeting place for artists of the time. Trying to imitate the cabaret of the

This famous painting by Ramon Casas has adorned the main hall of the modernist café *Els Quatre Gats* from the very beginning.

legendary Parisian venue, the bar had a lounge where puppet theatre performances, lectures, exhibitions, and other cultural and social events took place. The business was mostly comprised of Francophiles dressed in the most authentic Bohemian Parisian style. Melodies and songs were often heard, performed by Enrique Granados (1867-1916) and other musicians, including Isaac Albéniz (1860-1909), who occasionally visited the establishment. Rusiñol, Casas, Utrillo, Tomás Moragas (1837-1906), Pablo Picasso (1881-1973), Eugeni d'Ors (1881-1954), and many others gathered there, where they discussed new artistic trends and encouraged each other to keep going.

SOME INFO

On one of the walls in the lounge, a massive painting by Ramon Casas hung, depicting the painter and the café's owner pedalling a two-seater tandem bicycle. Currently, the painting can be seen at the *Museu Nacional d'Art de Catalunya* National (Art Museum of Catalonia).

The Creator of Iberona Alias Poble Espanyol

Miquel Utrillo was the one who persuaded Pere Romeu to open a bar on the corner of Montesió and Espolsasacs, today Magdalenes Street. The establishment was in the Casa Martí, designed by Lluís Puig i Cadafalch. Romeu's funds were provided by Utrillo himself, as well as Manuel Girona, Matías Ardeniz, and Ramon Casas.

Utrillo was a former painter and writer, not due to a lack of quality or technique, but because he claimed that at a certain point in his life, he had lost the ability to translate what his mind conceived onto canvas or paper. Highly empathetic, lively, and witty, he could involve everyone in the most diverse creative projects. He travelled to Paris with other regulars from *Els Quatre Gats* to immerse himself in the art scene of the City of Light. He fell in love with Suzanne Valadon, with whom he had a passionate love affair and acknowledged her illegitimate child as his own. Over the years, this child would become the famous French painter, Maurice Utrillo.

Poble Espanyol, created by Miquel Utrillo, Ramon Reventós, and Xavier Nogués.

About Vocabulry
Initially, the project of the *Poble Espanyol* had been named *Iberona*, but Primo de Rivera and his dictatorship opted for the title it carries now.

Together with Ramon Reventós (1892-1976), the first rationalist architect in Barcelona and the creator of Teatre Grec, and the artist Xavier Nogués (1873-1940), he conceived *Poble Espanyol*. To carry out this project, they travelled across Spain for a considerable amount of time with the intention of selecting architectural elements that could best represent the different peculiarities of the towns and cities of Spain.

The Group of Els Quatre Gats Launches a Magazine

Pere Romeu, Miquel Utrillo (1862-1934), and the writer Santiago Rusiñol (1861-1931) published a magazine with the name *Els Quatre Gats* (The Four Cats) - Artistic-Literary Publication. It was a four-page folio with a colourful cover and literary texts on the remaining pages. It was actually an attempt to advertise the business and had many contributors, including artists like Apel·les Mestres (1854-1936), Peius Gener, Eugeni d'Ors, Ramon Casas, Ramon Pichot (1871-1925), and Isidre Nonell (1872-1911), among many others.

Els Quatre Gats only published 15 issues between the months of February and May 1899. It was the precursor to *Pèl & Ploma*, a magazine that became indispensable for the dissemination of art news. It would eventually become a well-known and prestigious publication where Casas' first posters would appear.

Covers of *Els Quatre Gats* and *Pèl & Ploma* magazines.

When Picasso Paid for Dinners with a Drawing

Pablo Picasso, who visited *Els Quatre Gats* every night, always sat at a table next to the stained-glass windows. He was accompanied by the painter Rafael Padilla and the sculptor Mateo Soto. The three of them worked in a tiny attic of a run-down house on Consulado Street. To cover the cracks and dampness, the Malaga artist had decorated the walls of the apartment with paint.

In the midst of the puppet shows and the laughter of curious bourgeois who came to see those eccentric characters from the world of the arts, Picasso would draw. At some point in the a

typical day, the painter would get up to auction off his sporadic drawings among those present, and with what he earned from that small haul, he would treat himself to dinner. His first significant commission came from Pere Romeu, who entrusted him with a portrait of his son. For Picasso, that job meant a windfall of twenty-five pesetas.

Poster of *Els Quatre Gats* painted by Picasso.

Did you know?
After the end of the Civil War, Picasso went into exile in France. The painter, much like Pau Casals (1876-1973) and Josep Carner (1884-1970) would, never returned to Spain as a symbol of his staunch anti-Franco stance.

An eccentric with talent who enjoyed himself

Santiago Rusiñol, a regular at *Els Quatre Gats*, was a painter, bohemian, playwright, and storyteller. His aesthetic concepts had a significant influence on modernist ideas, although his painting showed a strong influence of French Impressionism. During his trips to Paris, Rusiñol maintained contact with painters and intellectuals who would influence his concept of art. Despite his artistic assertiveness, he was ironic, fun-loving, and at times, irresponsible and absurd in his personal life.

Santiago and women

Rusiñol had money and good looks, making him quite a catch. Many young women who visited *Els Quatre Gats* tried to win his heart, but they were never successful.

Café Montmartre (Montmartre Café), by Santiago Rusiñol, and El Greco's *Maria Magdalena,* a painting Rusiñol purchased in Paris to bring to Cau Ferrat in Sitges, where it can be admired today.

Among them, there were whispers that he was elusive due to greed. It's said that to a friend who asked him what he thought about her getting married, he replied: "Keep in mind that love fades, but marriage endures".

The Legacy of a Hugely Famous Figure in Sitges

A remarkable event in his artistic life was the discovery of El Greco (1541-1614). In Paris, he bought two paintings by the artist and brought them to Cau Ferrat, his home in Sitges. The arrival of the paintings in the town caused such a procession of friends and acquaintances who wanted to closely admire the acquisitions that some of the local villagers believed that a European celebrity had arrived at Rusiñol's house. People thought, at the very least, that he was a nobleman, and some even speculated that he might be a prince. In Sitges, during those days, everyone kept an eye on Cau Ferrat in case they were lucky enough to catch a glimpse of the famous European personality.

The Sculptor of Modernist Jewels

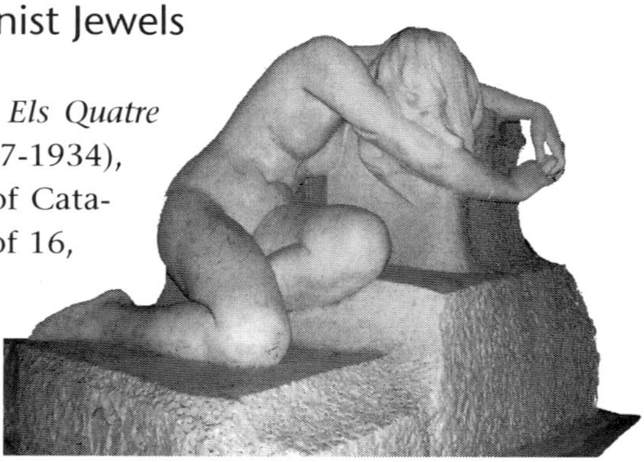

Another frequent visitor to *Els Quatre Gats* was Josep Llimona (1867-1934), one of the finest sculptors of Catalan modernism. At the age of 16, while studying in Rome on a scholarship, he created the equestrian statue of Ramon Berenguer the Great, which is now located in the square named after the count.

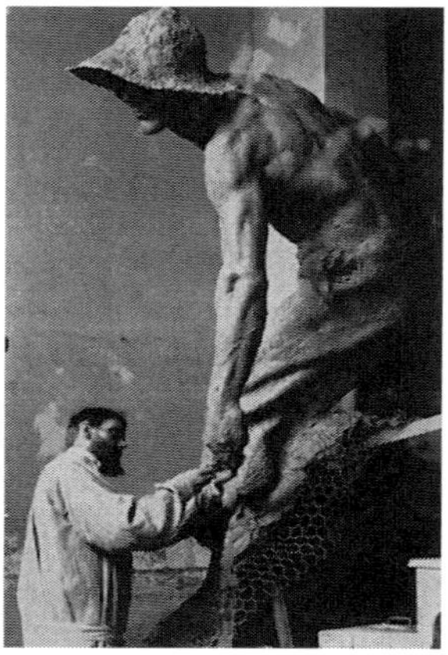

Josep Llimona sculpted the famous *Desconsol* (Heartbreak) sculpture above in tribute to his wife.

One of his most special monuments is *Desconsol* (Heartbreak), created after the disappearance of his wife following ten years of marriage. The statue, which can be seen in the middle of the pond in Ciutadella Park, was the first female nude in a long series that the sculptor would undertake.

Llimona created emotionally expressive funerary art, making him the preferred sculptor of the bourgeoisie for family mausoleums. He also dedicated himself to designing some jewellery. In fact, many of the goldsmith pieces sold today as modernist are copies of his designs.

The Pablo Gargallo Museum, in Zaragoza.

The Pioneer of Iron Sculpture

Pablo Gargallo (1881-1934) was another great sculptor who would frequently visit *Els Quatre Gats*. He was the pioneer of iron sculpture. Both Gargallo and Llimona collaborated on almost all the works of modernism with sculptures, balconies, reliefs, and medallions.

SOME INFO

In the current *Bosque de la Rambla del Prat* cinema, there are four reliefs created by the artist: one corresponds to himself, and the other three represent Ramon Reventós, Picasso, and Isidre Nonell.

The Painting That Became Famous Due to a Bourgeois's Attack

Isidre Nonell, the painter of poverty.

Isidre Nonell (1872-1911) was one of the most vibrant personalities of *Els Quatre Gats*. Among all the painters of the time, Nonell was the boldest and most powerful.

In 1900, he exhibited a painting at the Sala Parés. A bourgeois who had just come from church entered the room, and upon seeing the painting, was left speechless. Unable to understand why a gallery like Parés was displaying a painting that depicted the destitute and gypsies living on the outskirts of Barcelona with great realism, highlighting the filth, poverty, and the pungent landscape that surrounded them, the man tore the canvas with his umbrella amid curses and insults. The incident quickly spread by word of mouth, and from that day on, Isidre Nonell became a prominent figure in the Catalan art scene at the time.

Nonell discovered, from the beginning of his career, the aesthetic of the ugly and tragic. He lived among his models, sharing meals and drinks with them. He died very young, at the age of thirty-nine, from typhus. His funeral was attended by his friends and the marginalised people of Barcelona, who considered him one of their own. Six mourners, amid cries and lamentations, accompanied the coffin. The bourgeois attendees didn't complain because, after all, they had accepted that Nonell was the painter of poverty.

When Advertising Became Art

Advertising poster by Ramon Casas.

Ramon Casas, one of the founders of *Els Quatre Gats*, was such a regular attendee that some claim he didn't miss a single night in the seven years the tavern was open. Casas is one of the most important and well-known painters of the early 20th century. He shared his activities and exchanged ideas and projects with Utrillo, Rusiñol, Mestres, d'Ors, and other artists and intellectuals of the time. He travelled to Paris with Utrillo and Rusiñol to experience the new trends everyone was talking about. There, he discovered a new way to reach the public: through posters. Casas became a great poster artist, much like Toulouse Lautrec across the English Channel.

Some of his most famous posters were created for *Anís del Mono*, *Ámbar*, or *Espuma de Codorniu*. He managed to blend the relationship between art and commercial ideas without succumbing to simplicity, as he rigorously maintained his style in lines while intensifying the colour.

Casas and the Lottery Girl

One of the most shocking gossip stories of the time was Ramon Casas's marriage to one of his models. When Mrs. Casas found out that her son had married a lottery ticket seller, she couldn't bear it. She took it to heart to such an extent that she banned the young woman from the family home for many years.

SOME INFO

It's worth noting that Ramon Casas only created the advertising poster for *Anís del Mono* and not the label, which was the subject of much criticism. Casas' poster features a woman holding a small monkey by the hand, which, in turn, holds a bottle of anise under its arm. The controversial label on the bottle was designed by the owner's father-in-law and depicts a monkey with a human-like face, bearing a remarkable resemblance to Darwin.

The Soundtrack of the Tertulias

Another illustrious visitor to *Els Quatre Gats* was Isaac Albéniz (1860-1909). Of very humble origins, he had a challenging childhood despite being recognized as a child prodigy at an early age. At the age of four, he made his debut as a concert pianist in Barcelona and enjoyed great success, but the doors of the grand theatres wouldn't open to him until many years later.

It was Felip Pedrell (1841-1922) who convinced Albéniz to use Spanish music to create his own distinctive style. This is how success came to him in his maturity. In 1886, with the *Suite Española* (Spanish Suite), he initiated an unprecedented style of recreating folk music based on the purest canons of classical music. With this uniqueness, he became a musician with a distinctive identity, later triumphing with the *Suite para piano Iberia* (Suite for Iberian piano). His dream of creating "national music with universal appeal" had been realised.

Did you know?
Albéniz's admired compositions inspired musicians such as Manuel de Falla, Enric Granados, and Achille-Claude Debussy.

The Most Successful Musician

Enric Granados (1867-1916) possessed talent and, unlike Albéniz, was blessed with success from the very beginning. His first significant concert in Spain took place at the Lírico Theatre in Barcelona on April 19, 1890. Ten years later, he established the Granados Academy, which soon became a reference point for aspiring artists.

Enric Granados.

His masterpiece was *Goyescas,* which earned him immediate global recognition. It is said that during the creation of the work, Granados said to Pau Casals: "I've done something in bad taste, vulgar in the eyes of the public. I've created a 'jota' Aragonese dance". Casals' response was: "Perfect, wasn't Goya Aragonese?"

The last time Granados performed *Goyescas* was in New York, shortly before his death on the Sussex, a ship that sank following an attack. Pau Casals, accompanied by other internationally acclaimed artists, held a tribute concert for the maestro at the Metropolitan, the same place where Granados had triumphed just days before. The farewell to the great musician was performed by the Polish pianist Ignacy Jan Paderewski, who played Chopin's Funeral March with the audience standing and the theatre in darkness. There was only a candleholder near the piano.

The One Who Discovered Margarita Xirgu

Rafael Moragas was the first cultural promoter in Barcelona. He was enthusiastic by nature and had an immense capacity for promoting cultural activities. Alongside his inseparable friend Julio Vallmitjana, both passionate about theatre, they organised and staged several plays that would enthral a wide section of society.

One of the plays they decided to bring to the stage was Moragas' own translation of Émile Zola's *Thérèse Raquin.* With rehearsals well underway and the set almost complete, the leading actress of the play fell ill. With the show about to premiere, the cancellation meant frustration and a significant financial problem.

But as luck would have it, one of the actors suggested a visit to an amateur theatre. He said that on Sundays, there was a girl who "showed promise". The next day, Moragas and Vallmitjana visited the theatre and offered the leading role to the young girl. She replied that she was just an amateur and couldn't perform the role convincingly. When they told her that it didn't matter if she messed up, the girl agreed to act in exchange for five shillings. The premiere, a few days later, was a success. The name of this amateur was Margarita Xirgu.

Margarita Xirgu.

García Lorca's Muse

Young Margarita Xirgu was not only an extremely versatile actress but also possessed remarkable daring and courage. Her bravery was evident early on when, at just twenty-two years old, she dared to perform Oscar Wilde's *Salomé,* even though Wilde was a recognized homosexual at that time. During the play, Margarita danced the dance of the seven veils with her belly exposed. Although the gentlemen were delighted, there was a major scandal. The play, the author, and the actress were condemned as indecent, and the show was taken off the bill. But Xirgu didn't back down and continued to perform other plays, proud and stubborn, scandalizing the timid bourgeoisie.

García Lorca, Margarida Xirgu, and Cipriano Rivas at the premiere of *Yerma* in 1934.

For ten years, she would be Federico García Lorca's favourite actress. She premiered *Mariana Pineda, Yerma,* and *Doña Rosita la soltera.* The author and actress formed an intense friendship and a complicit attitude towards the society that sometimes applauded them and sometimes repudiated them. In 1931, she performed *Fermín Galán,* by Rafael Alberti, an openly republican work.

Voluntarily exiled after the victory of the Franco dictatorship, she first lived in Chile, then in Argentina, and finally in Uruguay, where she directed the *Comedia Nacional* and the *Escuela Municipal de Arte Dramático* (Municipal School of Dramatic Art).

SOME INFO

Her last performance was in Boston, where she portrayed *Yerma,* by Federico García Lorca.

Did you know?
Margarida Xirgu moved to Uruguay, where she lived during the last twenty years of her life.

The Moment of *La Puñalada* The Stabbing Arrives

The golden era of *Els Quatre Gats* ended in 1904. The place became deserted because its animators had moved to other places in the city, where they continued their gatherings. Pere Romeu cut his hair and beard, closed the bar, and dedicated himself to the world of automobiles, one of his favourite hobbies.

A Very Cultural Puñalada Stabbing

Some of the artists who had frequented *Els Quatre Gats* found a good substitute in a café restaurant on the corner of Passeig de Gràcia with Rosselló. It was *La Puñalada,* a bar.

The actress María Guerrero and the painter Santiago Rusiñol were regulars at the *tertulia* at La Puñalada.

It had started as a tavern for the carters heading towards the Vila de Gràcia. Its original name was *Olímpic Bar* (Olympic Bar), but when someone died from a stab wound, the place changed its name forever.

From time to time, literati of the calibre of Ramon María del Valle-Inclán or Rubén Darío, and popular actresses like María Guerrero, would join Rusiñol, Morgades, or Francesc Pujols. The bar's location was ideal as the promenade was in vogue. The eccentric architecture of the building did the rest to make the bar one of the most remarkable of the era.

Years later, with the war long gone, new artists would meet at *La Puñalada*. However, the restaurant began to decline until it closed its doors shortly before the turn of the 21st century. Now, the premises are occupied by a bank branch.

SOME INFO

They say that Santiago Rusiñol used to stay at *La Puñalada* for discussions until well after five in the morning when he left the place and went to buy newspapers.

The Most International Figures of the City

Raquel Meller: the Paral·lel Goddess

On the corner where Paral·lel Avenue and Nou de la Rambla Street meet, across from the Arnau Theatre, there's a square with a fountain featuring the statue of a young woman offering violets to pedestrians. It's Raquel Meller Square, the queen of the golden years of Paral·lel.

Meller was born as Francisca Marqués López on 9th March 1888 in Tarazona. The daughter of a humble Aragonese blacksmith, she lived with her family in the Poble Sec neighbourhood when she was a child. She worked in a local dressmaking workshop where it's said she used to sing while working, with a soft voice full of expressive tones. She soon caught the attention of some of the era's vedettes who frequented the workshop. In February 1908, Francisca made her debut at La Gran Peña salon with the name La Bella Raquel. In no time, she moved on to better venues, and that's when she changed her name to Raquel Meller. In September 1911, she made her debut at the Arnau Theatre in Barcelona. From then on, her career was unstoppable.

During this time, she popularized songs like *La violetera* and *El relicario*, even though José Padilla hadn't composed them for her. The Paral·lel goddess knew how to interpret them with perfect expressiveness, making them such impactful tunes that her style still permeates Spanish music to this day.

The great actress Raquel Meller.

On How Raquel Influences the Tastes of the Bourgeoisie

The cuplé was a genre considered to be lower status, reflecting the tastes of the common folk seeking easy entertainment with a hint of spice in the venues of Paral·lel. However, Meller's ability to convey emotions transformed the perception of the cuplé to such an extent that it began to be well-received by the bourgeoisie, high society, and intellectuals of the era. Thus, she became a muse for many intellectuals, especially lyricists and poets who wrote songs upon songs for the new goddess.

A portrait of Raquel Meller by Joaquim Sorolla (1918). On the right, the cover that Time magazine dedicated to the artist.

The charisma of the star, temperamental, ambitious, and arrogant, was so compelling that in 1918, Joaquim Sorolla wished to paint her portrait. In 1919, Raquel triumphed in Paris, Argentina, Uruguay, and Chile. In the same year, she embarked on her career in silent cinema. She filmed in Spain and France, starring in *Rosa de Flandes* (Flanders under Felipe II), *Violetas imperials* (Imperial Violets), *Carmen*, *La tierra prometida* (The Promised Land), *Ronda de noche* (The Night Watch), and *Nocturno* (Night).

In 1926, she embarked on a grand tour of the United States, where the audience succumbed to the allure of the queen of Paral·lel, and she graced the cover of the seventeenth issue of Time magazine on April 26, 1926, an honour typically reserved for major international stars and politicians.

The Spanish Civil War and the Second World War disrupted the dreams and the future of all of Europe, and Raquel Meller's career was no exception. In 1937, she travelled to Argentina, where she stayed until 1939. After the Civil War, she returned to Barcelona and there, for the second time, she tied the knot with the French entrepreneur Demon Sayac, from whom she divorced in 1943. In the following years, the abrupt break in society due to the war and post-war period, along with the emergence of other artistic forms sound cinema, different rhythms, American comedy, etc., left Raquel Meller alone and forgotten in Barcelona. She had two adopted children to whom she didn't pay much attention, and it's said that she spent her final years surrounded by cats. She passed away in 1962.

A Catalan University Student in the 16th Century

Juliana Morell, the only woman to be recognised in the University of Barcelona's roll of honour.

Juliana Morell was born in 1594 on Cendra Street in the Raval neighbourhood, and she's the only woman mentioned in the University of Barcelona's roll of honour. As the daughter of a wealthy banker well-placed in Barcelona's society, she was sent to the Dominican convent at a young age because her mother had died during childbirth. When she was four, the Dominicans returned her to her father, believing she had already acquired all the knowledge the convent could offer. From then on, her father took it upon himself to provide her with an education befitting her intelligence. Humanist tutors and scholars meticulously shaped the education of this extraordinarily talented girl. At the age of seven, she was already proficient in Latin, Hebrew, and Greek. By twelve, she had mastered Spanish, Arabic, Syriac, Italian, and French, along with logic, morality, and the humanities. By seventeen, she could speak, read, and write in fourteen languages.

When she was seven or eight years old, her father was forced to flee Barcelona due to financial problems. Once settled in France, Juliana would participate in philosophical and theological debates before even turning fifteen. Her intelligence and dialectical ability would be recognised everywhere.

Juliana decided to join the Dominican order against her father's wishes. The man passionately opposed the idea, eventually withdrawing her dowry. However, a friend, the Countess of Conté, and some Church members including the Bishop of Avignon gathered enough money to endow her.

Despite their efforts, in the end, the money wouldn't be necessary. After long conversations with his daughter, the father accepted the path she had chosen. In the convent, Juliana dedicated herself entirely to knowledge. She would write, translate, and enjoy intellectual recognition.

SOME INFO

In *Laurel de Apolo* (1630), Lope de Vega dedicates some verses to Juliana Morell.

The Catalan Submarine Inventor

Narcís Monturiol.

The engineer Narcís Monturiol (1819-1885) studied law but would never practise as a lawyer. A republican and utopian socialist, his restless spirit led him to explore many fields, but above all, Monturiol was an inventor. When he was the director of the National Stamp Factory, he devised a system for drying gummed paper. He also designed a funicular tram, a system for transporting water from the Ter River in Barcelona, synthetic shoe soles, a machine for rolling cigarettes, and a

With the *Ictineu*, Narciso Monturiol managed to navigate underwater for two hours, accompanied by two other argonauts: Josep Missé, the helmsman, and Josep Oliu, Monturiol's first mate.

procedure for soap production. His greatest invention was a type of vessel that he named the *Ictíneo, el barco*.

Using the *Ictíneo*, he submerged several times in the port of Barcelona in 1858. The first time, he remained submerged for twenty minutes. After fifty-four dives, he succeeded in staying underwater for two hours. Monturiol had to work hard to solve some technical issues. The contraption, which was 13.5 meters long, was powered by a steam engine and a four-bladed propeller. It consisted of a wooden body inside a copper one and featured an observation turret and a hatch. The invention was presented to the authorities, who promised resources to Monturiol to develop it. However, the funds never arrived, and the *Ictíneo* ended up being sold as scrap. Some say its engine ended up in a flour factory.

El Poblenou or the Perfect Society

With industrialisation, so many factories were established in the former town of Sant Martí de Provençals that the area would eventually become the most industrially concentrated area in

Catalonia. Monturiol was a follower of utopian socialism, influenced by the French philosopher Étienne Cabet, who in his novel *Voyage en Icarie* described life on an island inhabited by an ideal communist society. Between 1846 and 1847, a group of people decided to live in a community according to Cabet's utopian ideals in a place they would call Poblenou (New Town). The founders of this future neighbourhood in Barcelona believed in the possibility of starting a better and kinder society. As a reminder of their attempt, the Cerdà Plan decided to name the avenue leading to the old Poblenou cemetery Icaria Avenue.

Étienne Cabet.

SOME INFO

Cabet put his ideas into practice and founded his desired *Icaria* in the United States. All Icarian settlements would quickly fail, except one in Iowa, which lasted until 1895.

Josep Anselm Clavé, the Man Who Encouraged Workers to Sing

You can't talk about utopian socialism in Barcelona without mentioning one of the city's most popular and emblematic figures: Josep Anselm Clavé (1824-1874). Born in the Ribera neighbourhood, he was a self-taught musician, poet, and politician. From a very young age, he frequented the cafes of Barcelona with a guitar, singing his own songs.

Statue of Clavé, on the Sant Joan promenade.

Sculpture by Anselm Clavé in the Palau de la Música Catalana. On the left, the famous Clavé Choirs, Spain's first choir, in 1892.

His talent opened doors and provided opportunities. One of them was the chance to lead a group of musicians. Named *La Aurora,* which he sang in cafes and gave serenades. He worked with them to make them sound really good, and thus, the first choir in Barcelona and in Spain was born in 1850. With this experience, Clavé found an activity in which he could bring together humble people with the only capital of their voice.

Choral singing would spread among the working class. Clavé tried to bring his choirs and dances to Passeig de Gràcia, but the bourgeoisie of Barcelona fiercely opposed him: they couldn't allow the common people to invade what had been their territory until then.

After some arrests caused by his republican political activism, he organised shows in the Euterpe Gardens with unprecedented success. He began publishing a pamphlet titled *Eco d'Euterpe,* which featured the programme of shows, cultural events, and literary excerpts.

The first time Wagner was performed in Spain was at the Liceu in Barcelona with the work Tannhäuser, sung by the women's choir of the Liceu, in 1863.

In 1860, the Associació Euterpense was founded, a gathering of the different choirs that had originated in the city.

Wagner for the first time in Barcelona

Two aspects need to be highlighted in Clavé's performance and initiatives: he promoted the associational movement and improved the use of the Catalan language. Clavé worked to instil self-esteem, group consciousness, and culture in the workers. As his prestige grew, the bourgeoisie took note to the extent that the women's choir of the Liceo, along with the euterpense choirs, performed passages from Richard Wagner's work *Tannhäuser*. It was the first time Wagner had been performed in Spain.

Josep Anselm Clavé.

In 1867, Clavé was arrested and deported again, this time to Madrid. But the momentum of the process he had set in motion was so great that nothing stopped: the choirs, the shows, the publications, the dances etc. everything continued. He returned in 1868 and, because of the revolution that overthrew Isabel II, he became involved in political activity. During the Revolutionary Sexennium, he was a deputy and president of the *Diputación de Barcelona* (Barcelona Municipal Council). When the Sexennium ended, Clavé returned to Barcelona and died two months later.

A Nobel Prize Winner Who Quietly Passed Through Barcelona

The scientist Santiago Ramon y Cajal (1852-1934) arrived in Barcelona in 1887 to take up the position of Histology professor at the University of Medicine in the city. It was here that he would continue his research on neurons and their function.

Santiago Ramon y Cajal.

This expert in histology and microscopic pathological anatomy, one of the world's best, lived on Notariat Street very short, barely an island where he made advances in his major discoveries. He resided in a modest flat where, with the precision that characterised his work, he spent his days creating perfect drawings on fine, yellow-toned paper. He himself considered 1888 to be his best year when he laid the foundations for the study of the morphology and connections of nerve cells, eventually developing what came to be known as the doctrine of neurons. Many people are unaware that it was in this house where the most significant step in neurological science for understanding the human brain took place.

Ramon y Cajal presented the *Theory of Neurons* in 1889, at just thirty-seven years old, during a congress of the German Anatomical Society in Berlin. In 1892, he moved to the Central University of Madrid. He was the leading figure of the *Generation of Wise Men*. In 1906, he was awarded the Nobel Prize in Medicine. He passed away in 1934, at the age of eighty-two, surrounded by his students, just as he had wished.

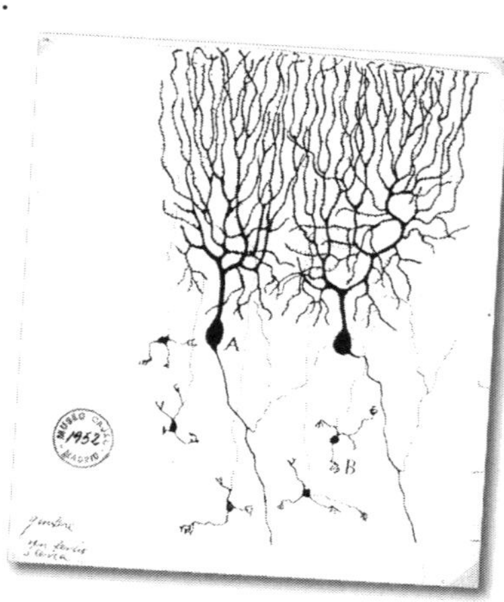

Drawing of Purkinje cells made by Santiago Ramon y Cajal in 1899.

Las señoritas de Avinyó (The Young Ladies of Avignon) Were from Barcelona

The old town of Barcelona is intricate. Amidst so many winding streets, you get the feeling that you are walking straight when, in fact, you are drifting. One of these impossible streets is particularly associated with the world of painting, thanks to a painting by Pablo Picasso: it's Avinyó Street, which starts at Ferran and, parallel to La Rambla, ends at Passeig de Colom. Avinyó was, before Picasso took any notice of it, a street occupied by a bourgeoisie that had yet to discover the grandeur of the Eixample.

The area surrounding the street is known as the Palau district because in 1378, the wife of Peter the Ceremonious, Leonor of Sicily, had a majestic building constructed on the site of a former Templar hostel. To distinguish it from the Palau Reial Major, located in Plaça del Rei, this new construction was named the Palau de la Reina or Palau Reial Menor. The building was demolished in 1856 due to its deterioration.

Avinyó Street, in Ciutat Vella, was the residence of the bourgeoisie at the beginning of the century.

Certainly, one of the things that initially appealed to the man from Malaga was the paper warehouse that was in the building now occupied by the Mercantile Casino. This business, almost the only one of its kind in Barcelona, attracted anyone in need of paper for their work. In fact, the store was so important that the street was popularly known as *Pape Street*. But the place had other features that must have also caught the young painter's attention. One of them: brothels everywhere.

Self-portrait of Pablo Picasso.

The Young Ladies of Avignon (1906-1907), by Pablo Picasso.

To Each His Own Name

In the spring of 1907, Picasso completed a painting that would be a turning point in his work, though for art history, it would signify a major departure. The painting, featuring five naked women, spent its early years without any title.

It turns out that it was a common practice for the painter to take his time naming his work. When Picasso first showed the canvas to his friends, he had not yet christened it. Although there is no written evidence to prove it, it is said that the French critic André Salmon was the one who named what we now know as *Les Demoiselles d'Avignon*. With this name, Salmon did not intend to refer to any particular town in his country, but it was a direct reference to a street in Barcelona. This street, in addition to having a paper shop, had several brothels scattered along its long silhouette. However, ignorance is quite daring, and since the Malagueño's Barcelona adventures were only known within his circle of friends, the name *Avinyó* soon began to be confused with the Gallic *Avignon*. The ladies in that painting didn't speak with an affected accent; they spoke Catalan fluently. We should be respectful of them because these women unwittingly became the mothers of a new style: Cubism.

The Details of a Painting That Broke with the Past

Art theorists consider *Les Demoiselles d'Avignon* as the boundary between classical and modern painting. On the canvas, which is quite large 224 x 234 cm, we can see five naked women offering themselves to an invisible client in a brothel. In some of the sketches, Picasso toyed with the possibility of including two men, clearly indicating the sexual exchange theme of the painting. In the end, however, he changed his mind, and without the male presence, the story remained more diluted.

One of the early sketches of the painting.

What is now considered Picasso's most famous painting wasn't particularly well received at first. Matisse considered it the death of painting, Braque said it was like drinking oil while eating a burning wick, and Derain predicted Picasso's suicide. So, it can be said that it wasn't a very encouraging start.

Some scholars believe that this is the work in the history of art that has the most preliminary studies. Picasso spent almost half a year in his studio making over eight hundred sketches.

After its purchase in 1939 for $28,000, *Les Demoiselles d'Avignon* is now on display at the MOMA in New York.

A Curious Detail about George Orwell's Plaque.

A British Writer Captivated by Barcelona

George Orwell.

Eric Arthur Blair was George Orwell's real name (1903-1950). His most famous work, in which profound critiques of Soviet Stalinism can be found, are *Animal Farm* and *1984*. The latter novel introduced the concept of *Big Brother.* However, Orwell didn't just fight against injustices. The writer moved to Catalonia in the early days of the Spanish Civil War as a journalist and ended up joining the Republican militias to combat the fascists. His experiences in Catalonia and on the Aragon front gave rise to the book *Homage to Catalonia*, a heartfelt chronicle of the saddest and most uncertain days of Barcelona.

SOME INFO

Ironically, in the square that bears his name in Barcelona, you can see signs announcing the presence of surveillance cameras within a radius of five hundred metres. Big Brother, perhaps?

A Child, a Pumpkin, and a Perfect Personal Technique

Pau Casals was born in El Vendrell in 1876. At the age of five, he would accompany his father to the church where his father played the organ. The child soon began to learn to play the instrument, and before long, he was already collaborating with his father in the creation of simple compositions.

Casals displayed his talents at a very early age: he joined the church choir and learned to play the violin and the piano when he was just a child. He discovered the cello at a performance by travelling musicians. Its sound had such an impact on him that he constructed his own cello from a pumpkin, producing sounds and melodies that were difficult to conceive.

Pau Casals, one of the greatest Catalan musicians of all time.

From that moment, he knew it would be the instrument of his life. The musician developed a technique based on naturalness and freedom. He performed at the Royal Albert Hall in London with resounding success. But after a

Did you know?
Among his notable works are the oratorio *El pessebre* (1960), the *Himno a las Naciones Unidas* (1971), and, above all, *El cant dels ocells* (The Song of the Birds), an emotional piece that takes its melody from a Catalan folk theme and is known worldwide today.

On November 13, 1961, Pau Casals was invited by John Fitzgerald Kennedy to perform a concert at the White House.

week of concerts, the musician decided never to return to Great Britain due to the country's passivity in the face of Franco's tyranny.

The name of Pau Casals is inseparably linked to the cello. However, in addition to being a remarkable cellist, he was a skilled pianist, conductor, and a respected composer. He made history for his virtuosity and his stance in the world he lived in. He used his fame to tirelessly advocate for democracy, freedom, and the rights of the less fortunate.

As an orchestra conductor, he founded the Pau Casals Orchestra in Barcelona in 1920. The defeat of the republican cause in the Spanish Civil War forced him into exile. He would never return to Spain, passing away in Puerto Rico in 1973.

Paint and discover:

Relax with mandalas to color:

You can visit our website
www.redbookediciones.com
to see all our books:

You can follow us on:

redbook_ediciones

@Redbook_Ed

@RedbookEdiciones